D1544083

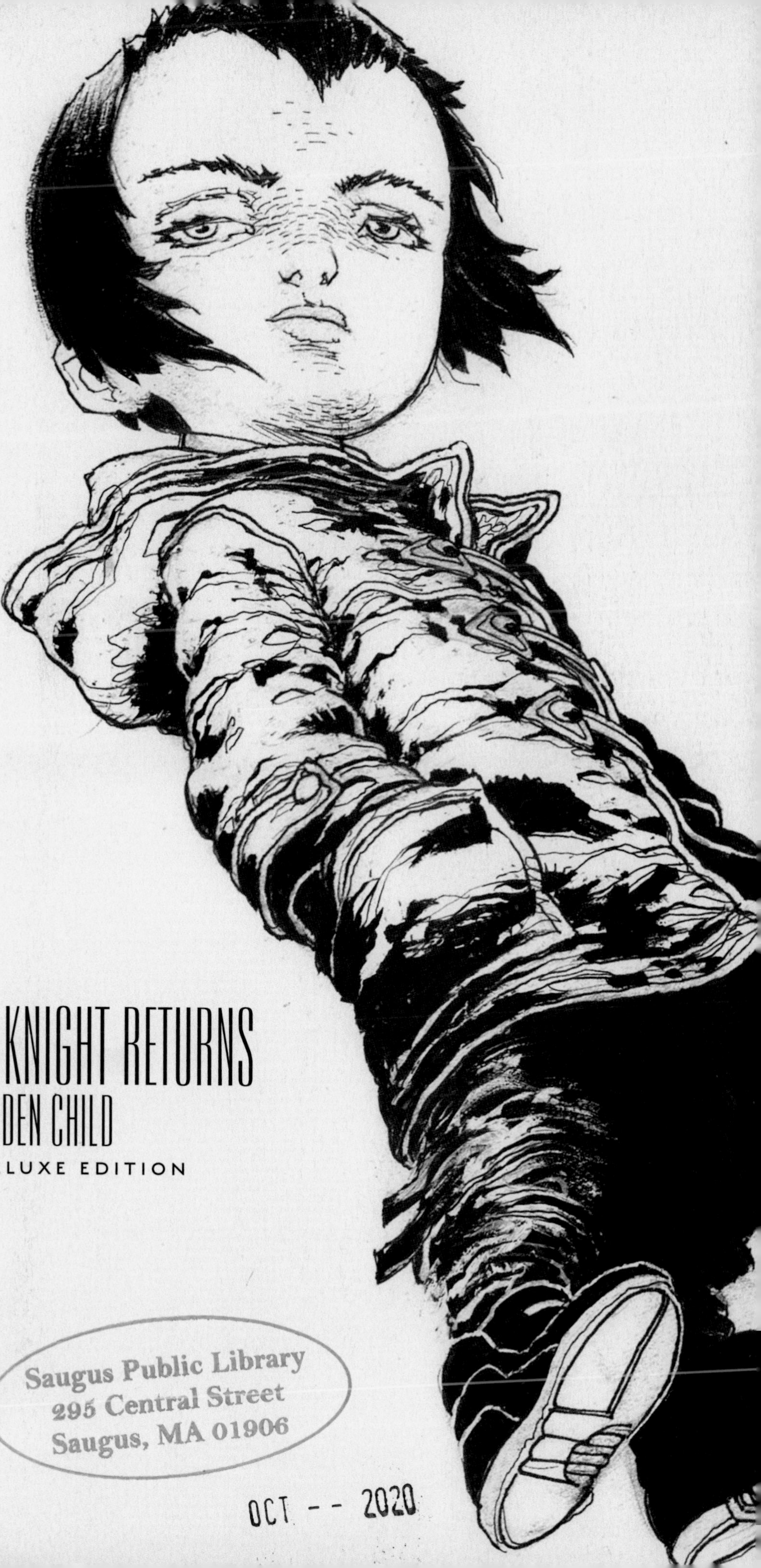

DARK KNIGHT RETURNS
THE GOLDEN CHILD
THE DELUXE EDITION

FRANK MILLER
writer

RAFAEL GRAMPÁ
artist

JORDIE BELLAIRE
colorist

**JOHN WORKMAN
& DERON BENNETT**
letterers

**RAFAEL GRAMPÁ
with PEDRO COBIACO**
collection cover artists

DARK KNIGHT RETURNS
THE GOLDEN CHILD
THE DELUXE EDITION

BATMAN created by BOB KANE with BILL FINGER

Special thanks to STEVE MILLER • JEFF DANZIGER • NEAL ADAMS

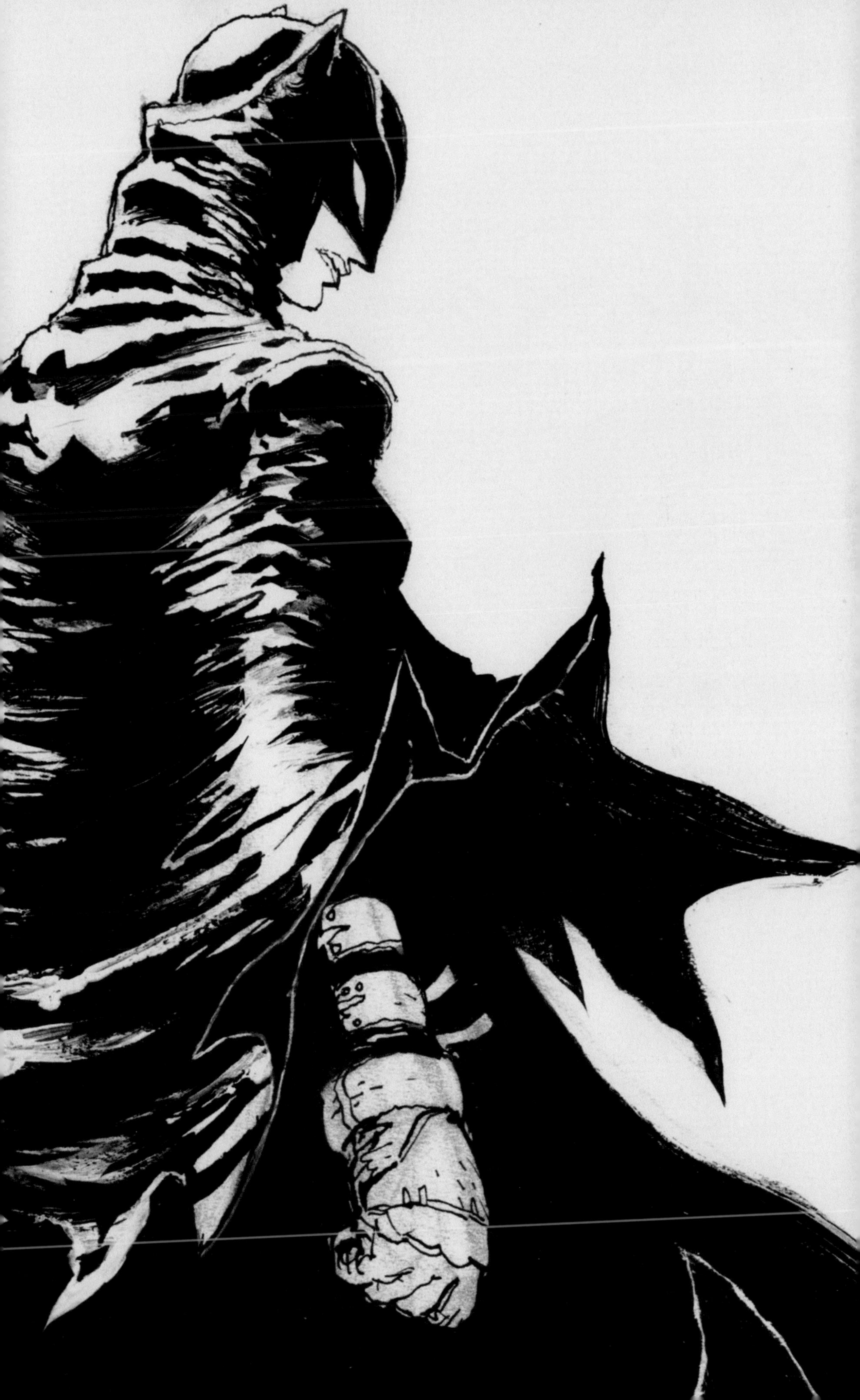

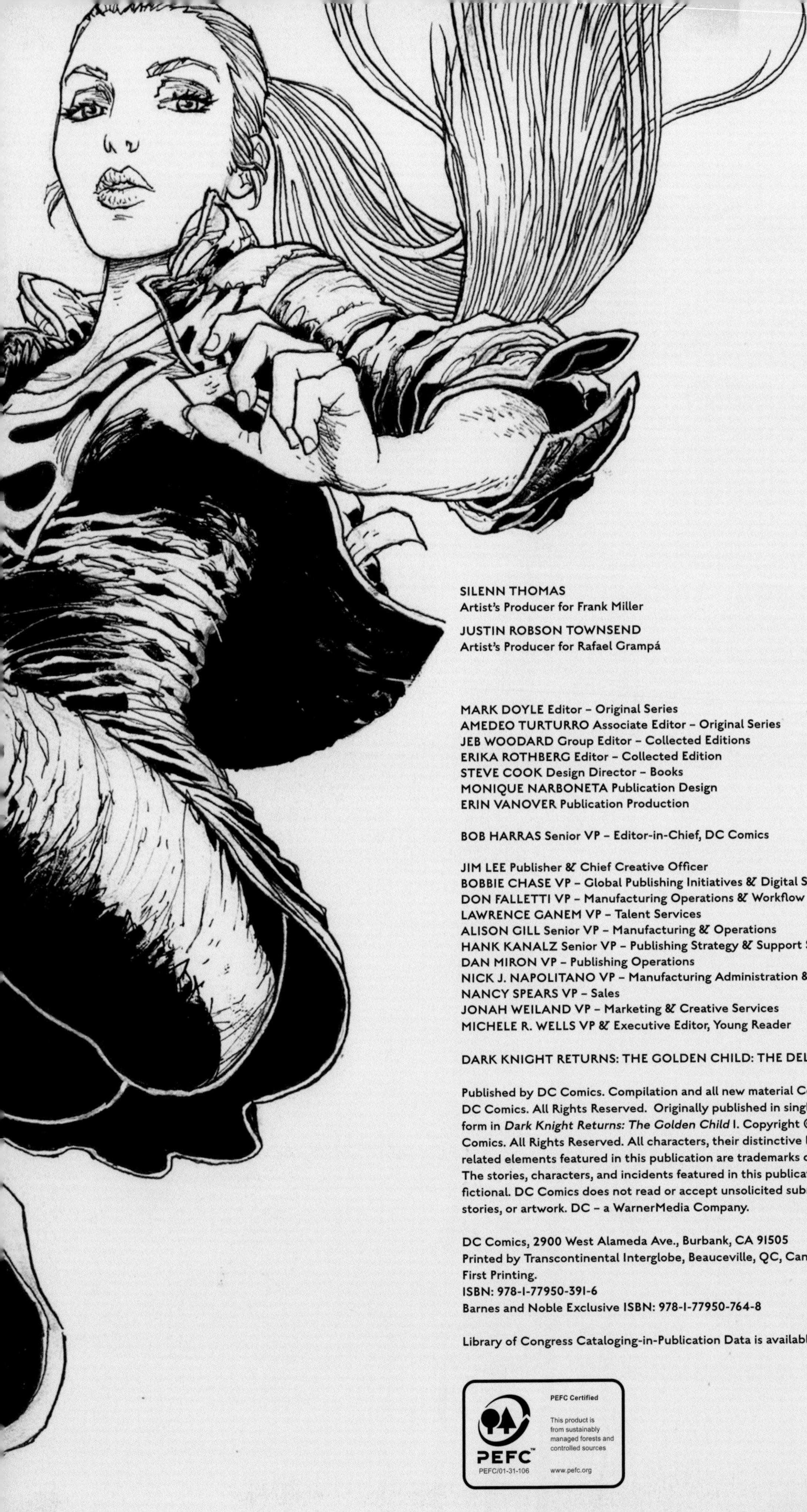

SILENN THOMAS
Artist's Producer for Frank Miller

JUSTIN ROBSON TOWNSEND
Artist's Producer for Rafael Grampá

MARK DOYLE Editor – Original Series
AMEDEO TURTURRO Associate Editor – Original Series
JEB WOODARD Group Editor – Collected Editions
ERIKA ROTHBERG Editor – Collected Edition
STEVE COOK Design Director – Books
MONIQUE NARBONETA Publication Design
ERIN VANOVER Publication Production

BOB HARRAS Senior VP – Editor-in-Chief, DC Comics

JIM LEE Publisher & Chief Creative Officer
BOBBIE CHASE VP – Global Publishing Initiatives & Digital Strategy
DON FALLETTI VP – Manufacturing Operations & Workflow Management
LAWRENCE GANEM VP – Talent Services
ALISON GILL Senior VP – Manufacturing & Operations
HANK KANALZ Senior VP – Publishing Strategy & Support Services
DAN MIRON VP – Publishing Operations
NICK J. NAPOLITANO VP – Manufacturing Administration & Design
NANCY SPEARS VP – Sales
JONAH WEILAND VP – Marketing & Creative Services
MICHELE R. WELLS VP & Executive Editor, Young Reader

DARK KNIGHT RETURNS: THE GOLDEN CHILD: THE DELUXE EDITION

DC Comics, 2900 West Alameda Ave., Burbank, CA 91505
Printed by Transcontinental Interglobe, Beauceville, QC, Canada. 8/7/2020.
First Printing.
ISBN: 978-1-77950-391-6
Barnes and Noble Exclusive ISBN: 978-1-77950-764-8

Library of Congress Cataloging-in-Publication Data is available.

PEFC Certified
This product is from sustainably managed forests and controlled sources
PEFC/01-31-106
www.pefc.org

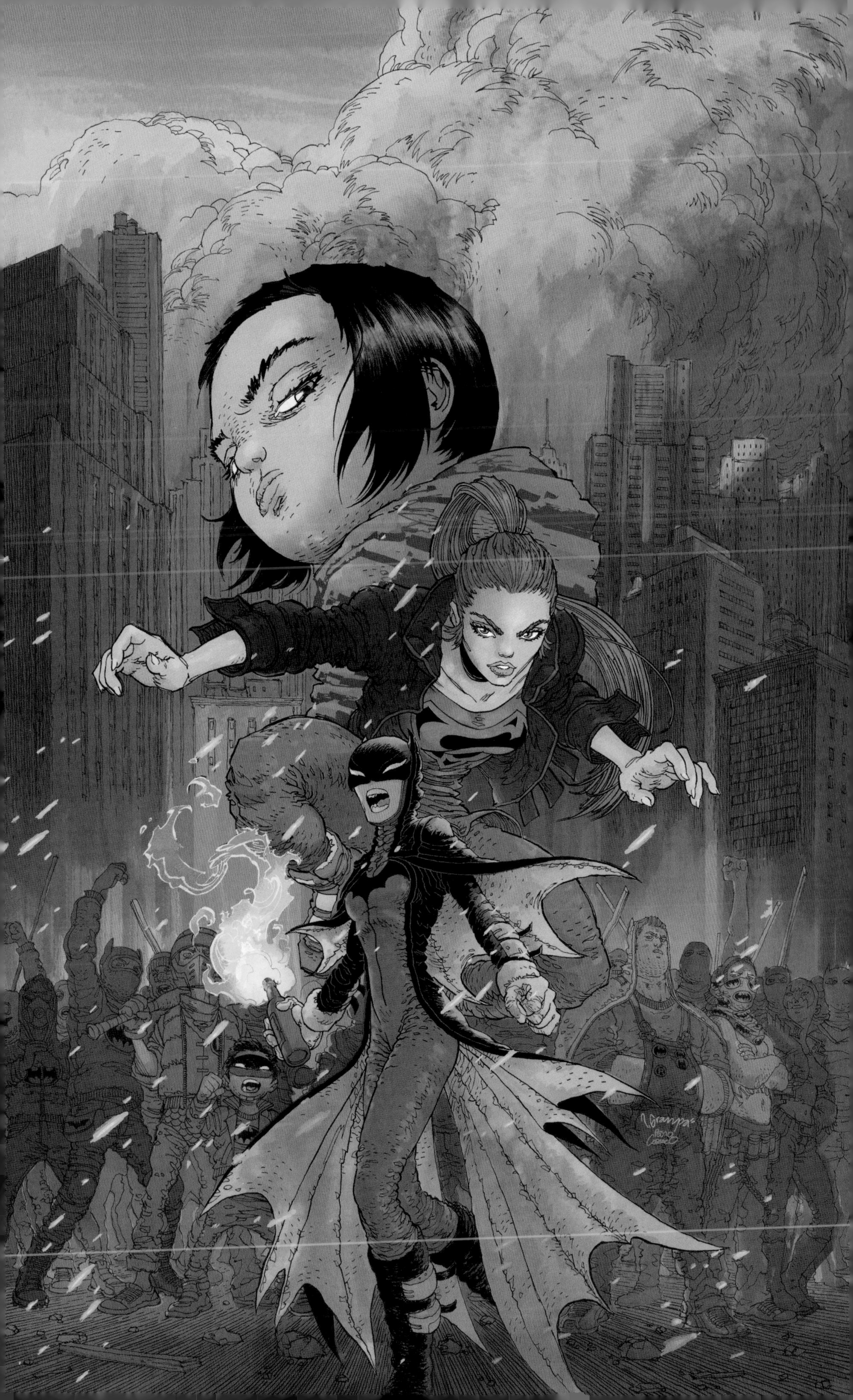

"This is going to be ugly.

This is going to be a mess.

This is going to be great."

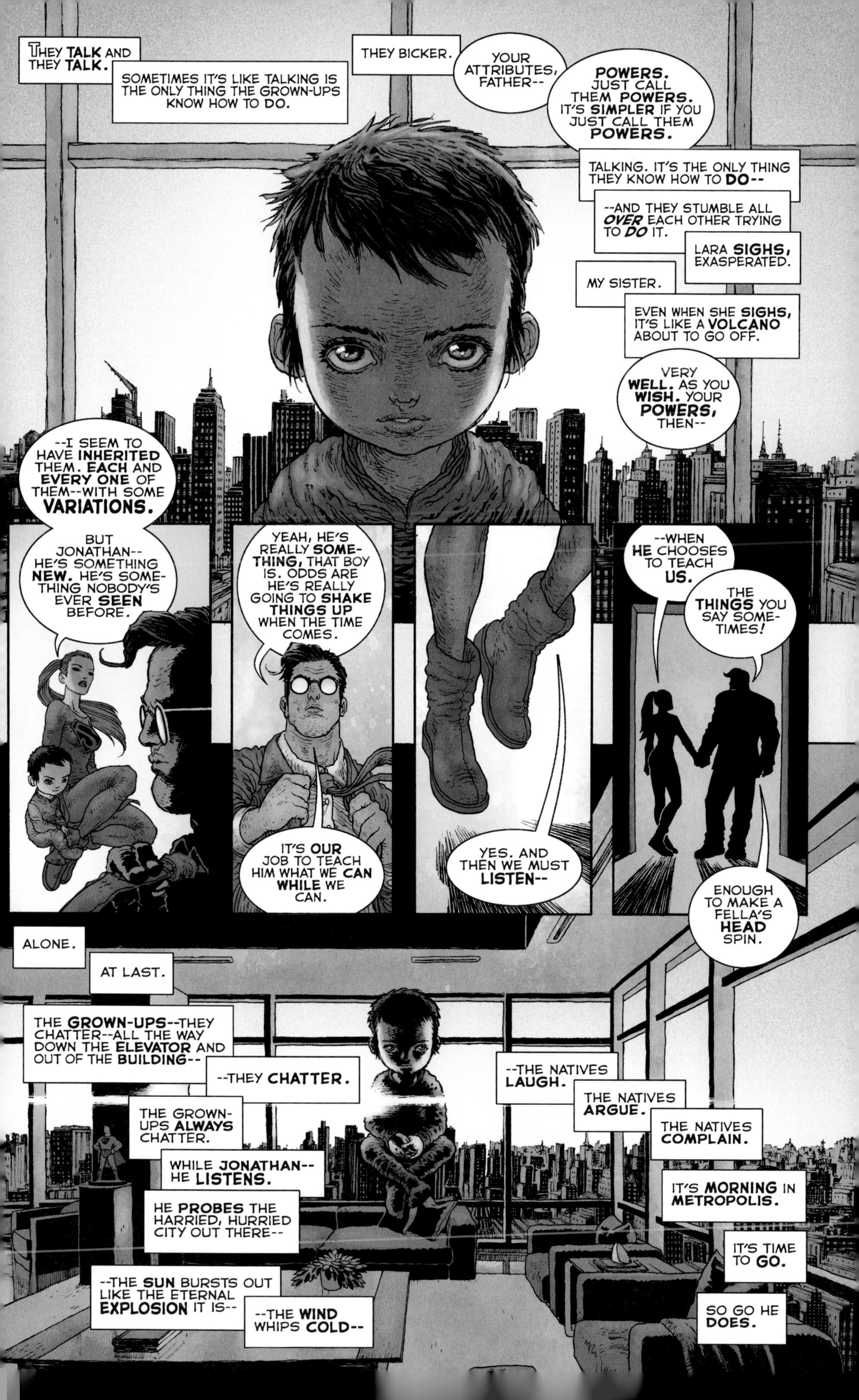
THEY TALK AND THEY TALK.
SOMETIMES IT'S LIKE TALKING IS THE ONLY THING THE GROWN-UPS KNOW HOW TO DO.
THEY BICKER.
YOUR ATTRIBUTES, FATHER--
POWERS. JUST CALL THEM POWERS. IT'S SIMPLER IF YOU JUST CALL THEM POWERS.
TALKING. IT'S THE ONLY THING THEY KNOW HOW TO DO--
--AND THEY STUMBLE ALL OVER EACH OTHER TRYING TO DO IT.
LARA SIGHS, EXASPERATED.
MY SISTER.
EVEN WHEN SHE SIGHS, IT'S LIKE A VOLCANO ABOUT TO GO OFF.
VERY WELL. AS YOU WISH. YOUR POWERS, THEN--
--I SEEM TO HAVE INHERITED THEM. EACH AND EVERY ONE OF THEM--WITH SOME VARIATIONS.
BUT JONATHAN-- HE'S SOMETHING NEW. HE'S SOMETHING NOBODY'S EVER SEEN BEFORE.
YEAH, HE'S REALLY SOMETHING, THAT BOY IS. ODDS ARE HE'S REALLY GOING TO SHAKE THINGS UP WHEN THE TIME COMES.
IT'S OUR JOB TO TEACH HIM WHAT WE CAN WHILE WE CAN.
YES. AND THEN WE MUST LISTEN--
--WHEN HE CHOOSES TO TEACH US.
THE THINGS YOU SAY SOMETIMES!
ENOUGH TO MAKE A FELLA'S HEAD SPIN.
ALONE.
AT LAST.
THE GROWN-UPS--THEY CHATTER--ALL THE WAY DOWN THE ELEVATOR AND OUT OF THE BUILDING--
--THEY CHATTER.
THE GROWN-UPS ALWAYS CHATTER.
WHILE JONATHAN-- HE LISTENS.
HE PROBES THE HARRIED, HURRIED CITY OUT THERE--
--THE SUN BURSTS OUT LIKE THE ETERNAL EXPLOSION IT IS--
--THE WIND WHIPS COLD--
--THE NATIVES LAUGH.
THE NATIVES ARGUE.
THE NATIVES COMPLAIN.
IT'S MORNING IN METROPOLIS.
IT'S TIME TO GO.
SO GO HE DOES.

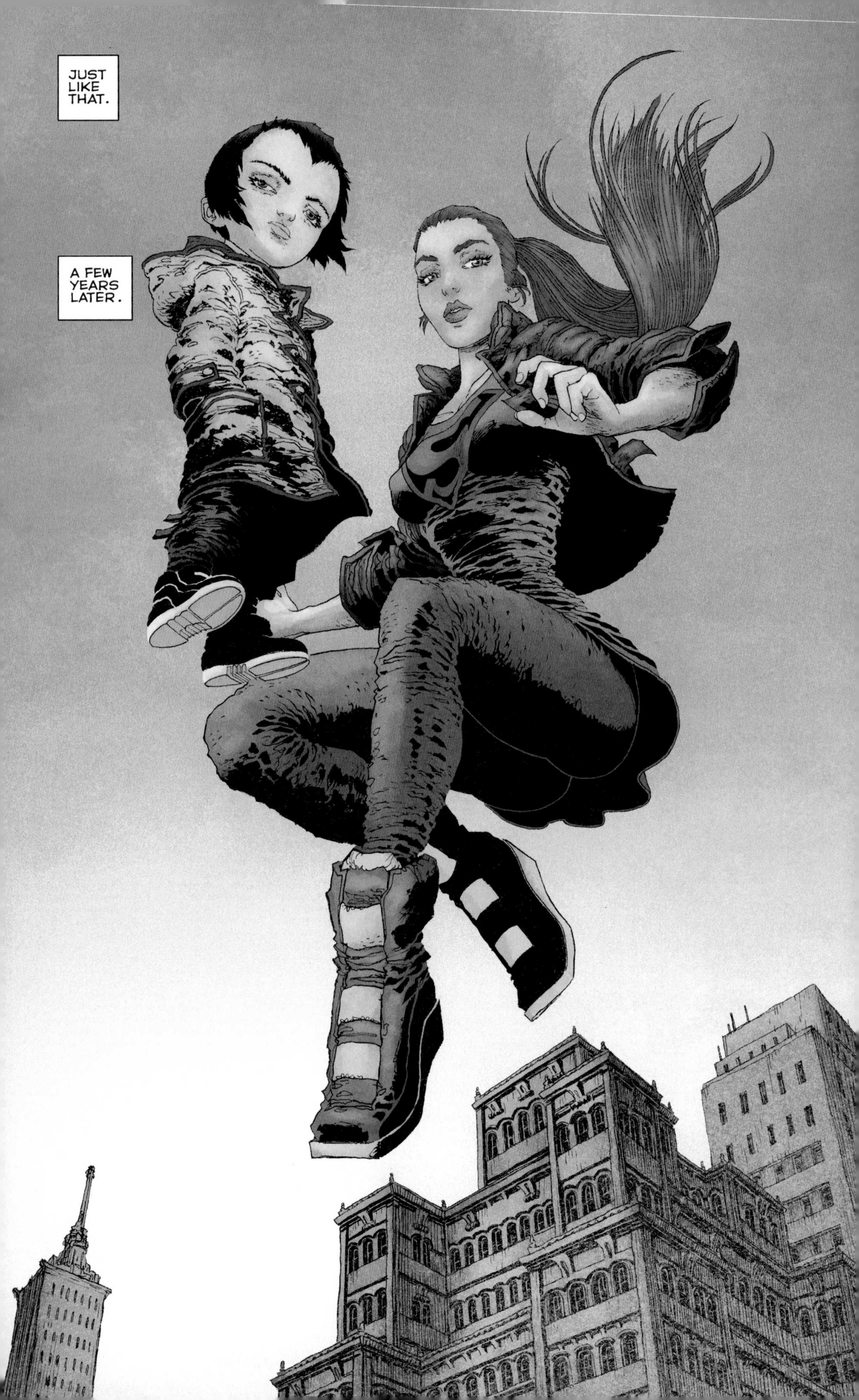
JUST LIKE THAT.
A FEW YEARS LATER.

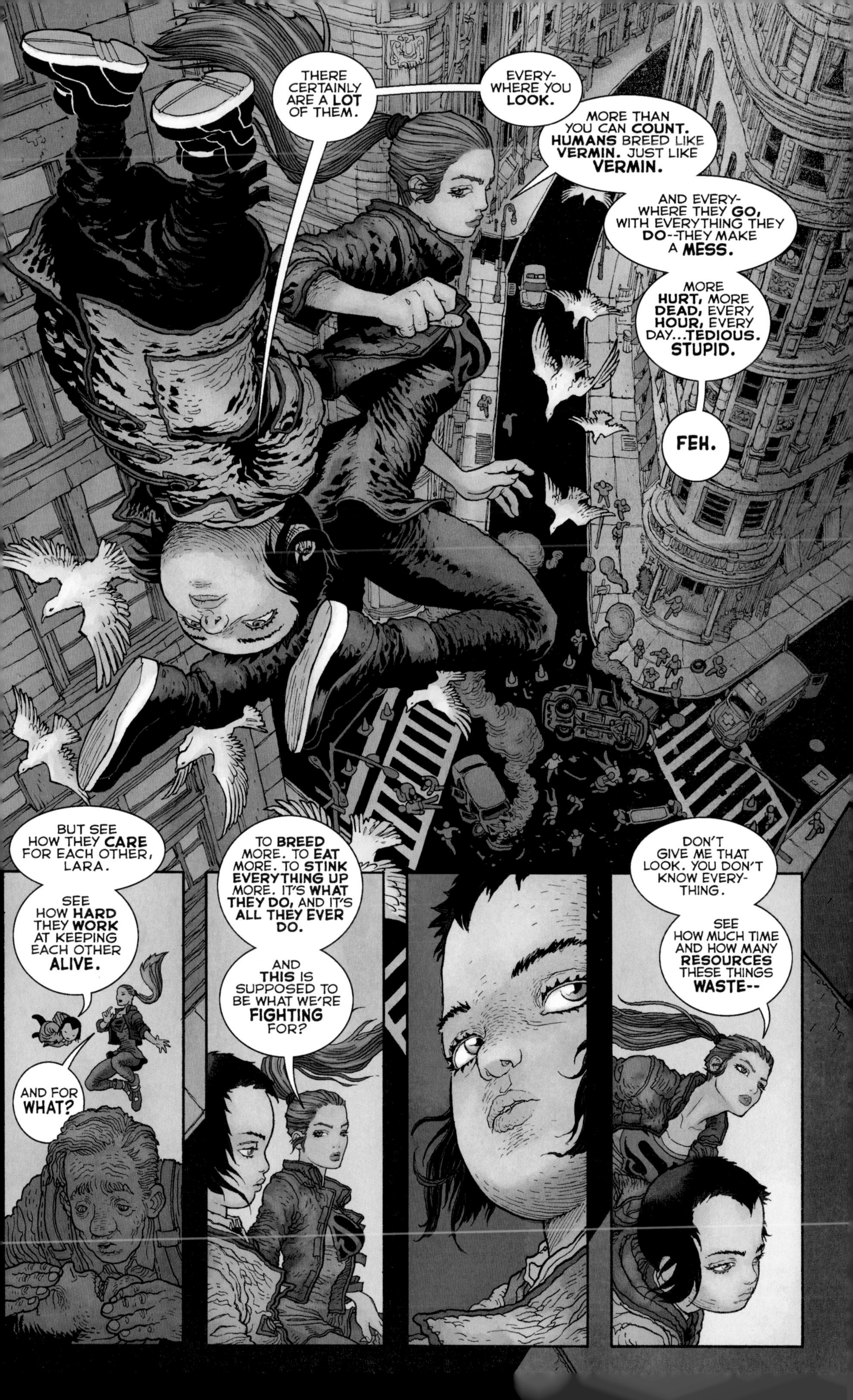
THERE CERTAINLY ARE A LOT OF THEM.
EVERY-WHERE YOU LOOK.
MORE THAN YOU CAN COUNT. HUMANS BREED LIKE VERMIN. JUST LIKE VERMIN.
AND EVERY-WHERE THEY GO, WITH EVERYTHING THEY DO--THEY MAKE A MESS.
MORE HURT, MORE DEAD, EVERY HOUR, EVERY DAY...TEDIOUS. STUPID.
FEH.
BUT SEE HOW THEY CARE FOR EACH OTHER, LARA.
SEE HOW HARD THEY WORK AT KEEPING EACH OTHER ALIVE.
AND FOR WHAT?
TO BREED MORE. TO EAT MORE. TO STINK EVERYTHING UP MORE. IT'S WHAT THEY DO, AND IT'S ALL THEY EVER DO.
AND THIS IS SUPPOSED TO BE WHAT WE'RE FIGHTING FOR?
DON'T GIVE ME THAT LOOK. YOU DON'T KNOW EVERY-THING.
SEE HOW MUCH TIME AND HOW MANY RESOURCES THESE THINGS WASTE--

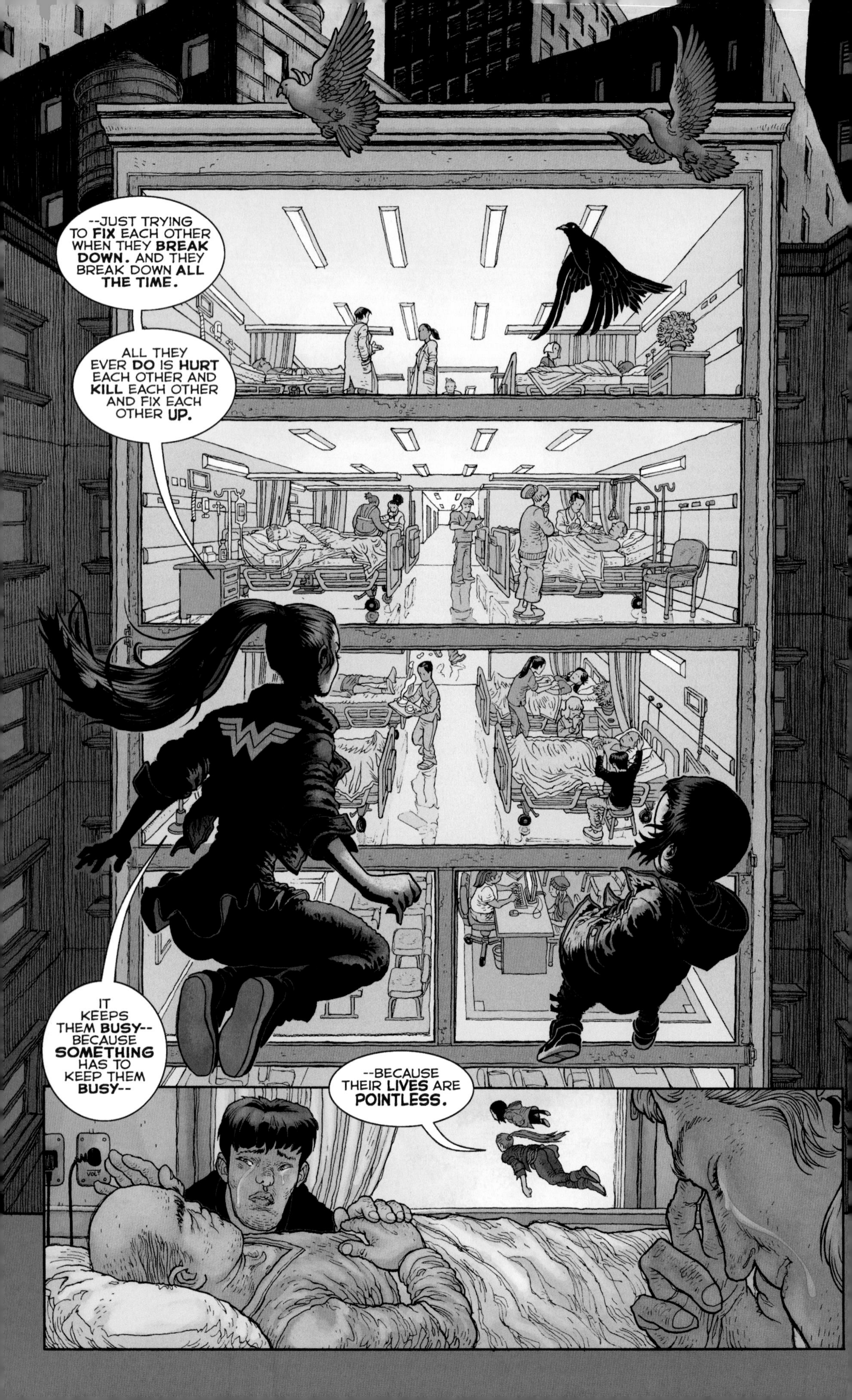
--JUST TRYING TO FIX EACH OTHER WHEN THEY BREAK DOWN. AND THEY BREAK DOWN ALL THE TIME.
ALL THEY EVER DO IS HURT EACH OTHER AND KILL EACH OTHER AND FIX EACH OTHER UP.
IT KEEPS THEM BUSY-- BECAUSE SOMETHING HAS TO KEEP THEM BUSY--
--BECAUSE THEIR LIVES ARE POINTLESS.

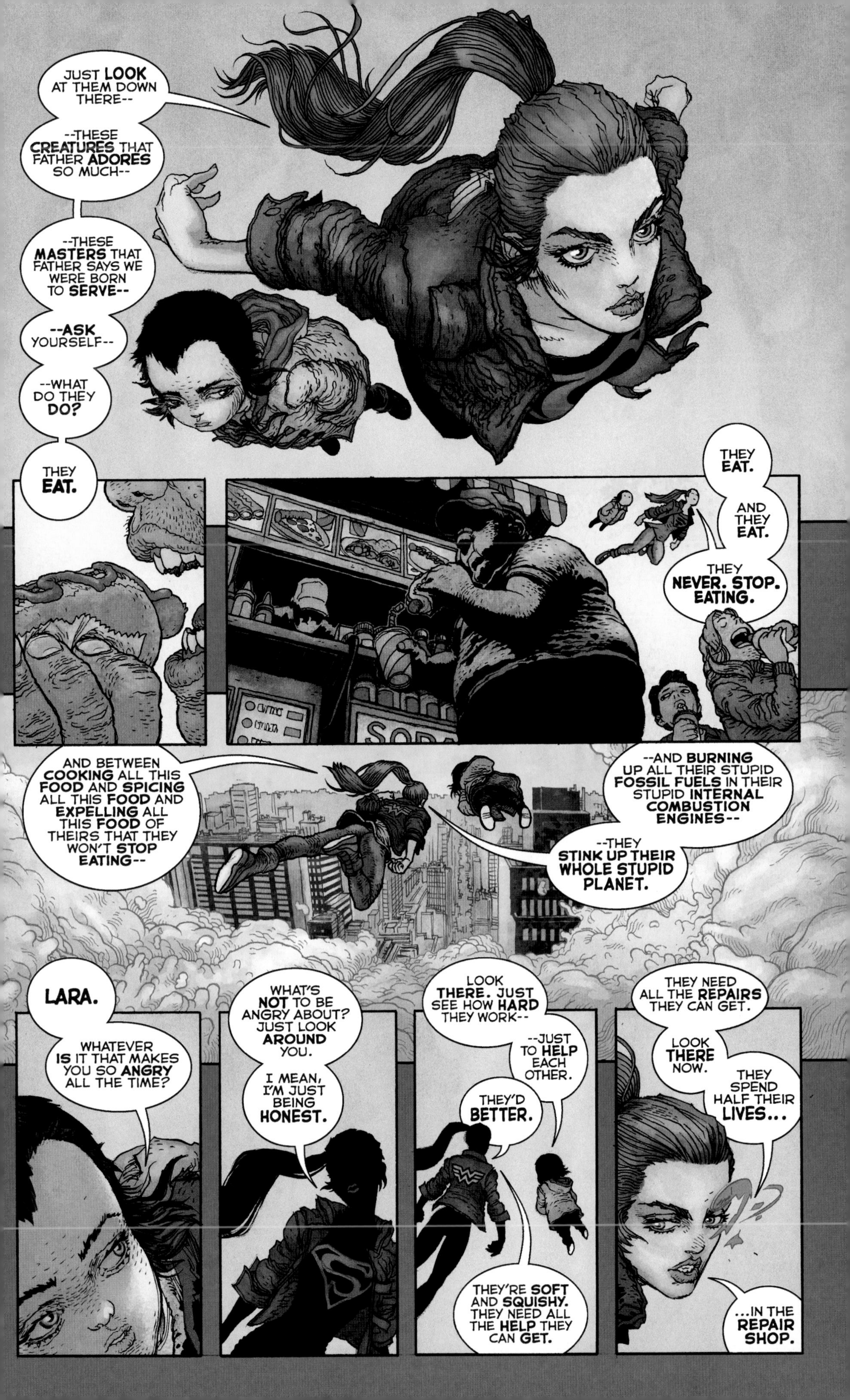
JUST LOOK AT THEM DOWN THERE--
--THESE CREATURES THAT FATHER ADORES SO MUCH--
--THESE MASTERS THAT FATHER SAYS WE WERE BORN TO SERVE--
--ASK YOURSELF--
--WHAT DO THEY DO?
THEY EAT.
THEY EAT.
AND THEY EAT.
THEY NEVER. STOP. EATING.
SODA
AND BETWEEN COOKING ALL THIS FOOD AND SPICING ALL THIS FOOD AND EXPELLING ALL THIS FOOD OF THEIRS THAT THEY WON'T STOP EATING--
--AND BURNING UP ALL THEIR STUPID FOSSIL FUELS IN THEIR STUPID INTERNAL COMBUSTION ENGINES--
--THEY STINK UP THEIR WHOLE STUPID PLANET.
LARA.
WHATEVER IS IT THAT MAKES YOU SO ANGRY ALL THE TIME?
WHAT'S NOT TO BE ANGRY ABOUT? JUST LOOK AROUND YOU.
I MEAN, I'M JUST BEING HONEST.
LOOK THERE. JUST SEE HOW HARD THEY WORK--
--JUST TO HELP EACH OTHER.
THEY'D BETTER.
THEY'RE SOFT AND SQUISHY. THEY NEED ALL THE HELP THEY CAN GET.
THEY NEED ALL THE REPAIRS THEY CAN GET.
LOOK THERE NOW.
THEY SPEND HALF THEIR LIVES...
...IN THE REPAIR SHOP.

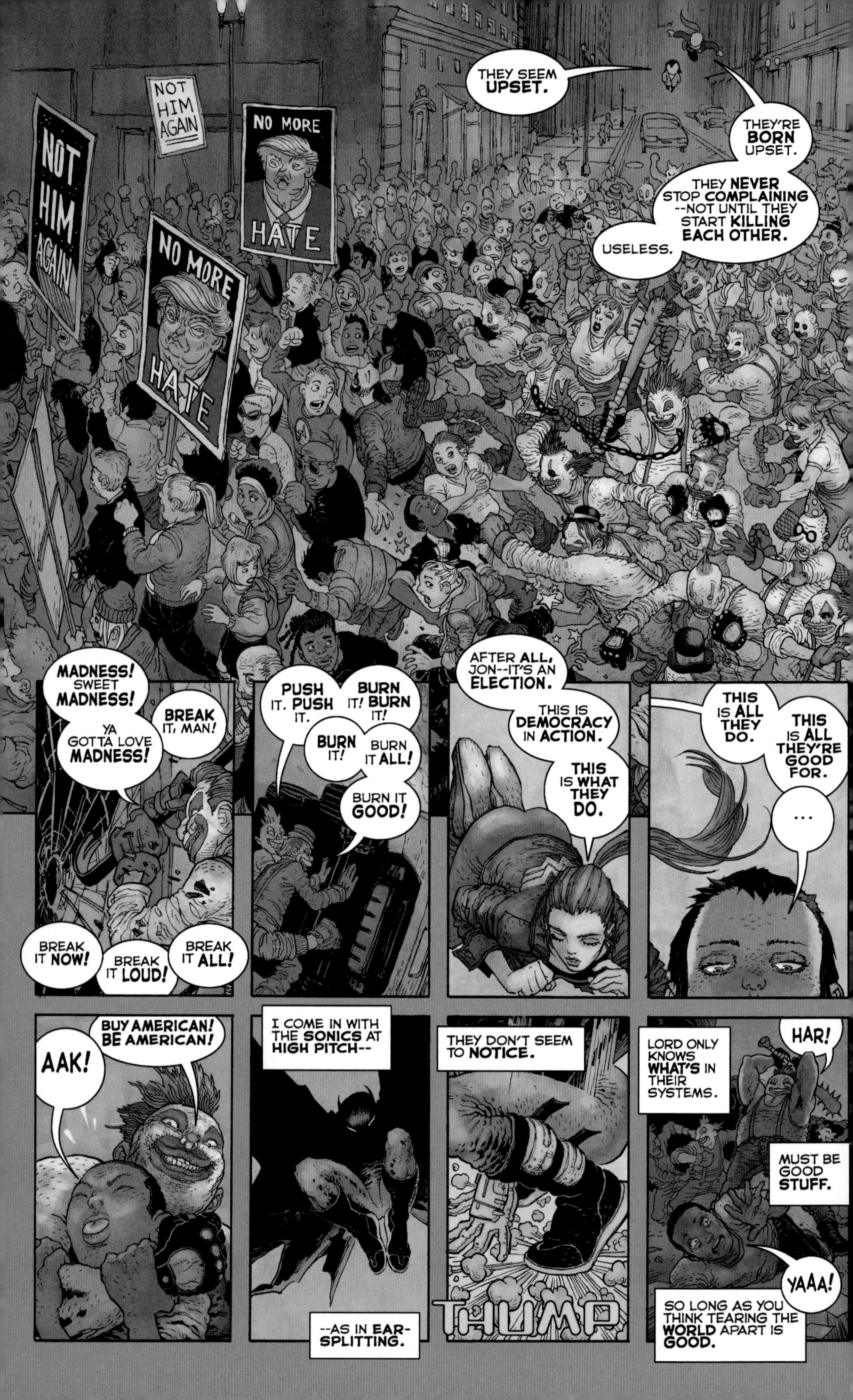
NOT HIM AGAIN
NOT HIM AGAIN
NO MORE HATE
NO MORE HATE
THEY SEEM UPSET.
THEY'RE BORN UPSET.
THEY NEVER STOP COMPLAINING --NOT UNTIL THEY START KILLING EACH OTHER.
USELESS.
MADNESS! SWEET MADNESS!
YA GOTTA LOVE MADNESS!
BREAK IT, MAN!
BREAK IT NOW!
BREAK IT LOUD!
BREAK IT ALL!
PUSH IT. PUSH IT.
BURN IT! BURN IT!
BURN IT!
BURN IT ALL!
BURN IT GOOD!
AFTER ALL, JON--IT'S AN ELECTION.
THIS IS DEMOCRACY IN ACTION.
THIS IS WHAT THEY DO.
THIS IS ALL THEY DO.
THIS IS ALL THEY'RE GOOD FOR.
...
BUY AMERICAN! BE AMERICAN!
AAK!
I COME IN WITH THE SONICS AT HIGH PITCH--
--AS IN EAR-SPLITTING.
THEY DON'T SEEM TO NOTICE.
THUMP
LORD ONLY KNOWS WHAT'S IN THEIR SYSTEMS.
HAR!
MUST BE GOOD STUFF.
YAAA!
SO LONG AS YOU THINK TEARING THE WORLD APART IS GOOD.

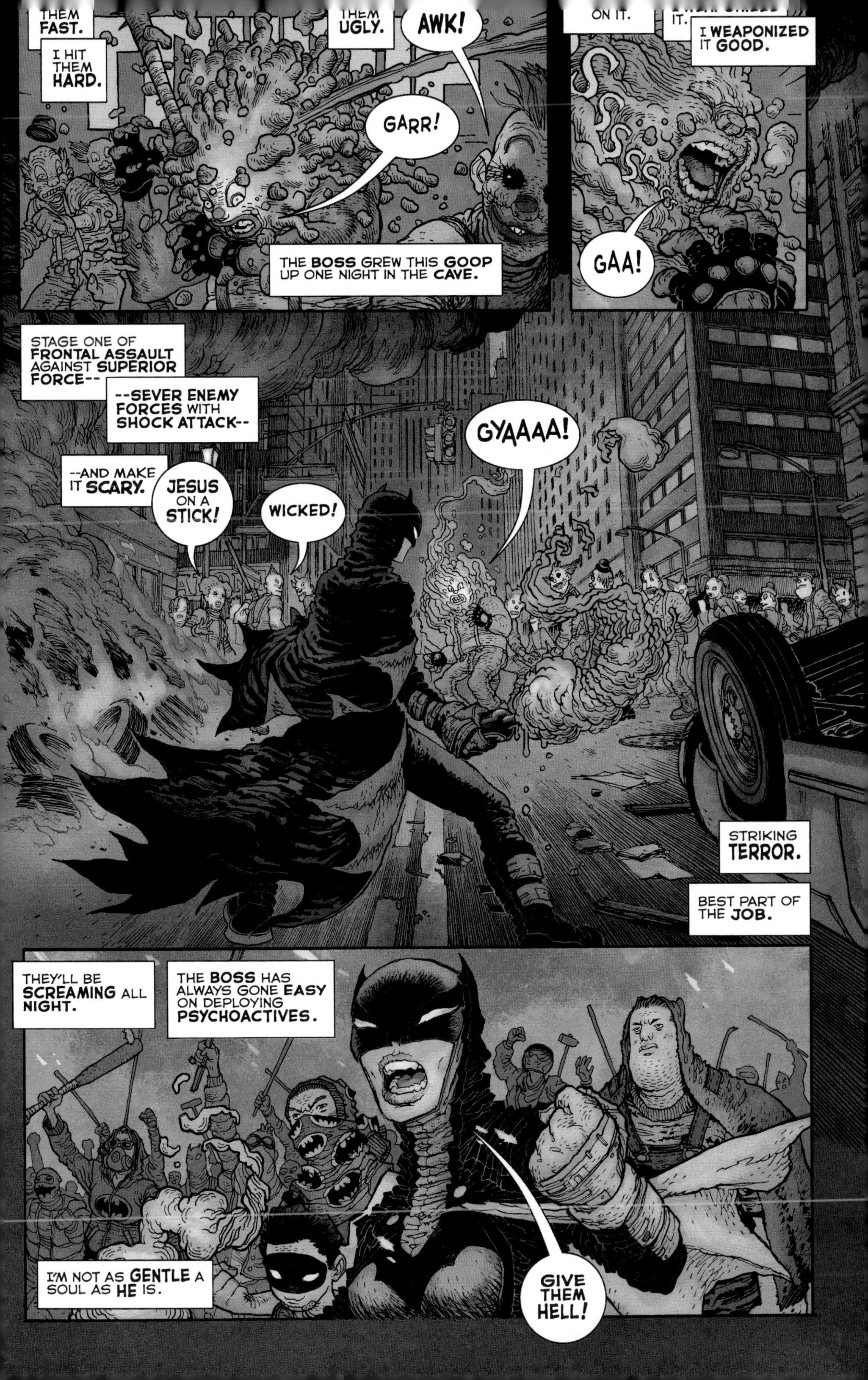

THEM FAST.
I HIT THEM HARD.
THEM UGLY.
AWK!
GARR!
THE BOSS GREW THIS GOOP UP ONE NIGHT IN THE CAVE.
ON IT.
IT.
I WEAPONIZED IT GOOD.
GAA!
STAGE ONE OF FRONTAL ASSAULT AGAINST SUPERIOR FORCE--
--SEVER ENEMY FORCES WITH SHOCK ATTACK--
--AND MAKE IT SCARY.
JESUS ON A STICK!
WICKED!
GYAAAA!
STRIKING TERROR.
BEST PART OF THE JOB.
THEY'LL BE SCREAMING ALL NIGHT.
THE BOSS HAS ALWAYS GONE EASY ON DEPLOYING PSYCHOACTIVES.
I'M NOT AS GENTLE A SOUL AS HE IS.
GIVE THEM HELL!

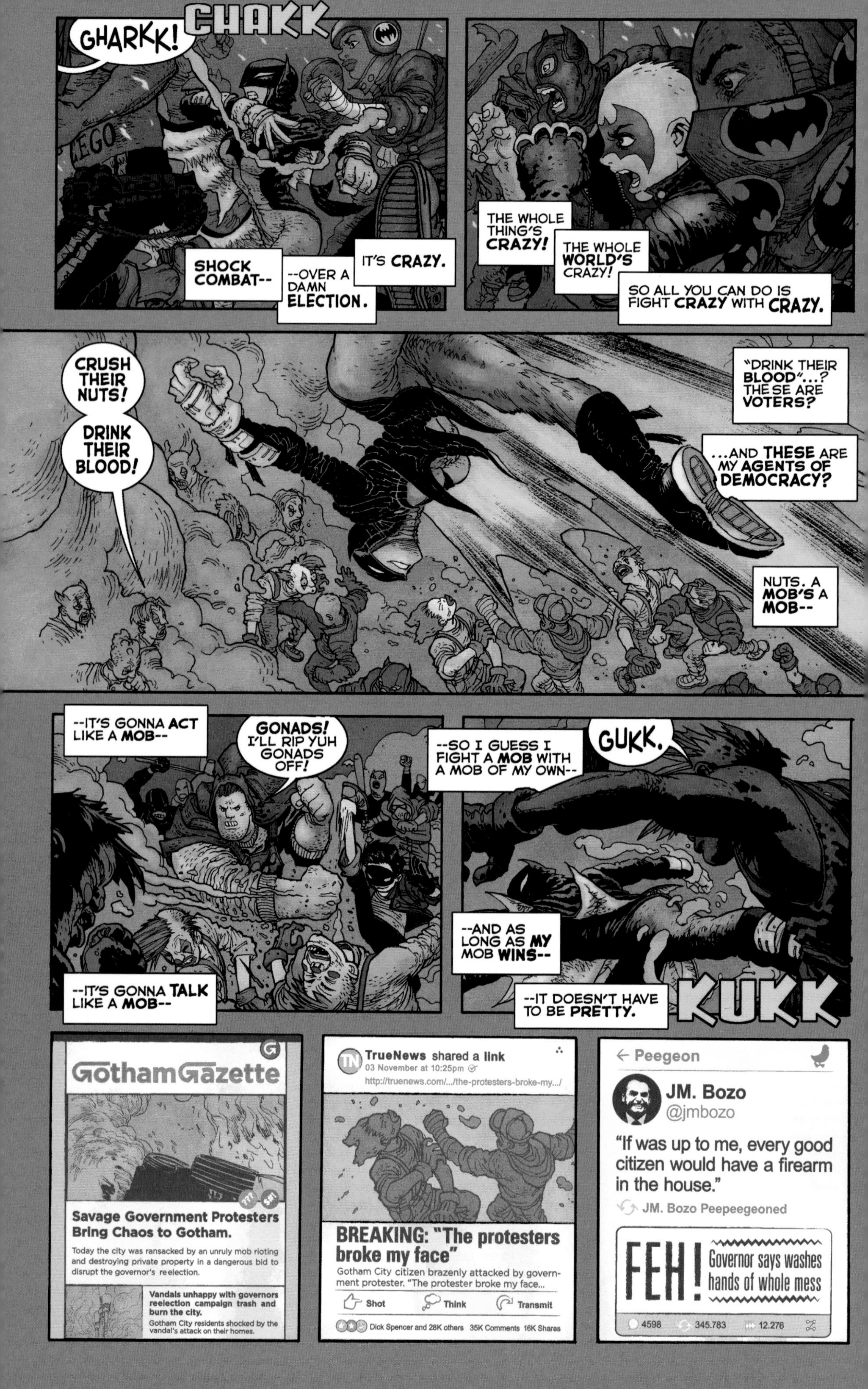

GHARKK!
CHAKK
SHOCK COMBAT--
--OVER A DAMN ELECTION.
IT'S CRAZY.
THE WHOLE THING'S CRAZY!
THE WHOLE WORLD'S CRAZY!
SO ALL YOU CAN DO IS FIGHT CRAZY WITH CRAZY.
CRUSH THEIR NUTS!
DRINK THEIR BLOOD!
"DRINK THEIR BLOOD"...? THESE ARE VOTERS?
...AND THESE ARE MY AGENTS OF DEMOCRACY?
NUTS. A MOB'S A MOB--
--IT'S GONNA ACT LIKE A MOB--
GONADS! I'LL RIP YUH GONADS OFF!
--IT'S GONNA TALK LIKE A MOB--
--SO I GUESS I FIGHT A MOB WITH A MOB OF MY OWN--
GUKK.
--AND AS LONG AS MY MOB WINS--
--IT DOESN'T HAVE TO BE PRETTY.
KUKK
GothamGazette
Savage Government Protesters Bring Chaos to Gotham.
Today the city was ransacked by an unruly mob rioting and destroying private property in a dangerous bid to disrupt the governor's reelection.
Vandals unhappy with governors reelection campaign trash and burn the city.
Gotham City residents shocked by the vandal's attack on their homes.
TrueNews shared a link
03 November at 10:25pm
http://truenews.com/.../the-protesters-broke-my.../
BREAKING: "The protesters broke my face"
Gotham City citizen brazenly attacked by government protester. "The protester broke my face...
Shot
Think
Transmit
Dick Spencer and 28K others 35K Comments 16K Shares
← Peegeon
JM. Bozo
@jmbozo
"If was up to me, every good citizen would have a firearm in the house."
JM. Bozo Peepeegeoned
FEH!
Governor says washes hands of whole mess
4598
345.783
12.276

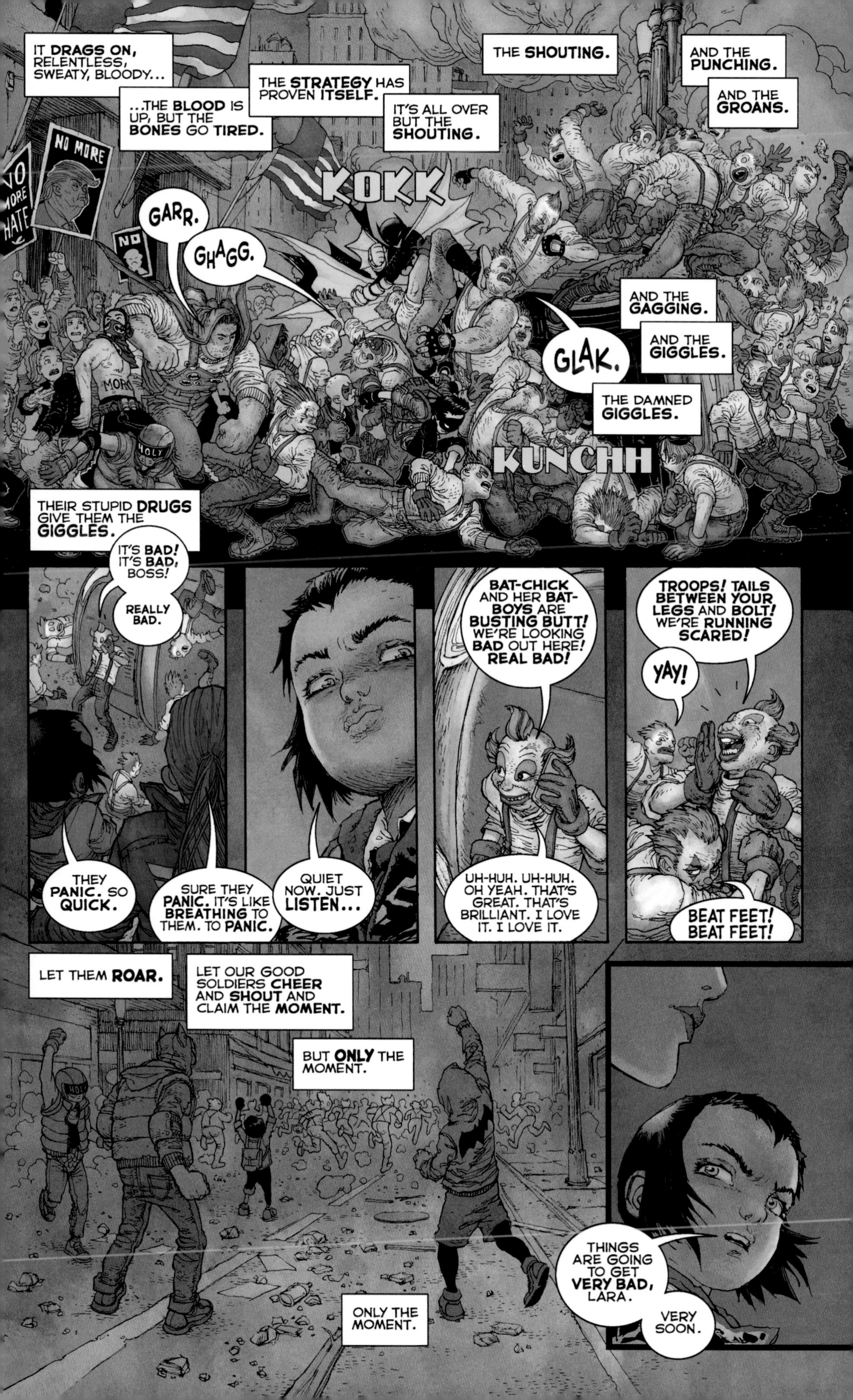
IT DRAGS ON, RELENTLESS, SWEATY, BLOODY...
...THE BLOOD IS UP, BUT THE BONES GO TIRED.
THE STRATEGY HAS PROVEN ITSELF.
IT'S ALL OVER BUT THE SHOUTING.
THE SHOUTING.
AND THE PUNCHING.
AND THE GROANS.
NO MORE HATE
NO MORE
NO
KOKK
GARR.
GHAGG.
MORE
HOLY
AND THE GAGGING.
AND THE GIGGLES.
GLAK.
THE DAMNED GIGGLES.
KUNCHH
THEIR STUPID DRUGS GIVE THEM THE GIGGLES.
IT'S BAD! IT'S BAD, BOSS!
REALLY BAD.
THEY PANIC. SO QUICK.
SURE THEY PANIC. IT'S LIKE BREATHING TO THEM. TO PANIC.
QUIET NOW. JUST LISTEN...
BAT-CHICK AND HER BAT-BOYS ARE BUSTING BUTT! WE'RE LOOKING BAD OUT HERE! REAL BAD!
UH-HUH. UH-HUH. OH YEAH. THAT'S GREAT. THAT'S BRILLIANT. I LOVE IT. I LOVE IT.
TROOPS! TAILS BETWEEN YOUR LEGS AND BOLT! WE'RE RUNNING SCARED!
YAY!
BEAT FEET! BEAT FEET!
LET THEM ROAR.
LET OUR GOOD SOLDIERS CHEER AND SHOUT AND CLAIM THE MOMENT.
BUT ONLY THE MOMENT.
ONLY THE MOMENT.
THINGS ARE GOING TO GET VERY BAD, LARA.
VERY SOON.

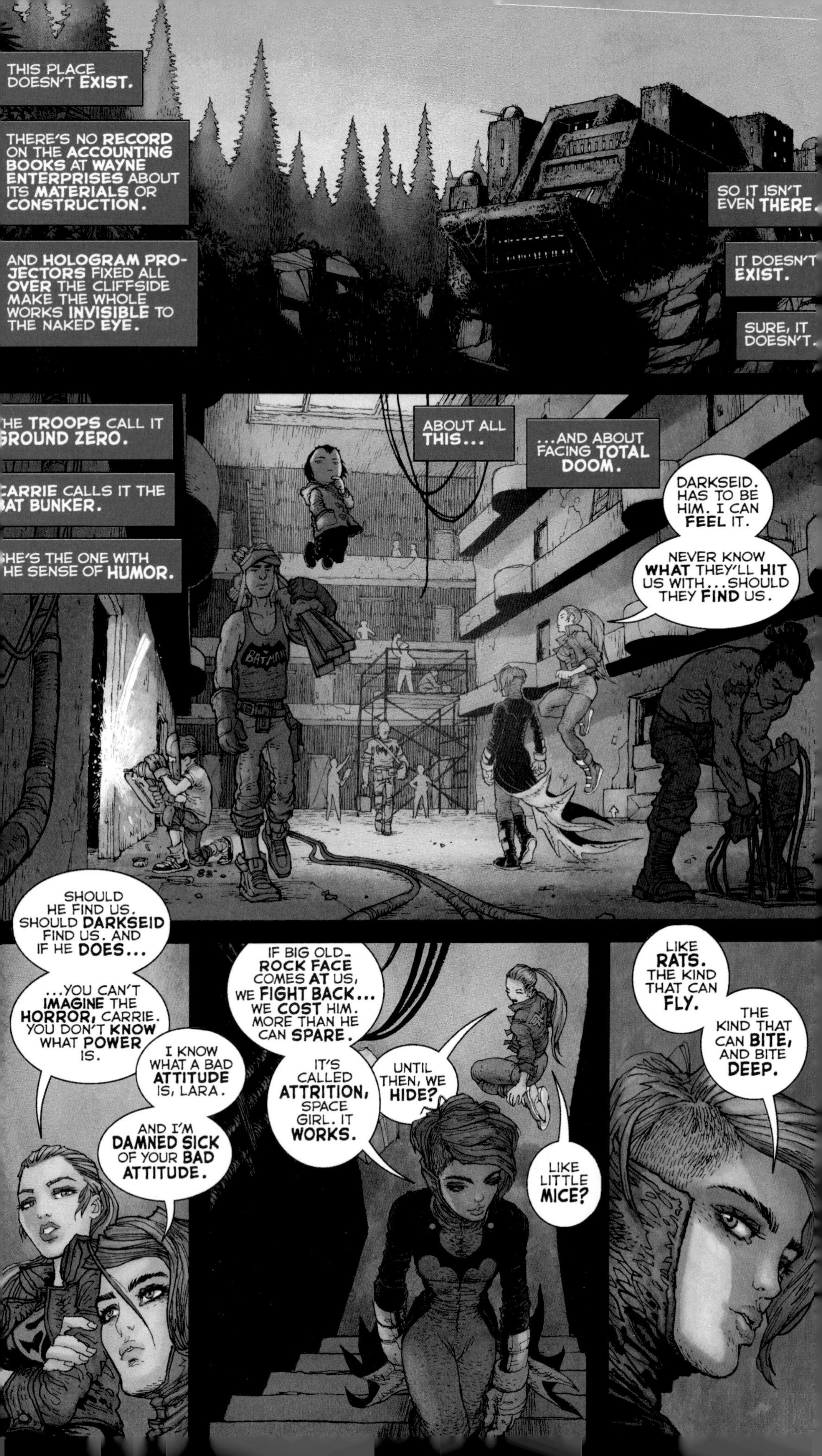
THIS PLACE DOESN'T EXIST.
THERE'S NO RECORD ON THE ACCOUNTING BOOKS AT WAYNE ENTERPRISES ABOUT ITS MATERIALS OR CONSTRUCTION.
AND HOLOGRAM PROJECTORS FIXED ALL OVER THE CLIFFSIDE MAKE THE WHOLE WORKS INVISIBLE TO THE NAKED EYE.
SO IT ISN'T EVEN THERE.
IT DOESN'T EXIST.
SURE, IT DOESN'T.
HE TROOPS CALL IT GROUND ZERO.
CARRIE CALLS IT THE BAT BUNKER.
SHE'S THE ONE WITH HE SENSE OF HUMOR.
ABOUT ALL THIS...
...AND ABOUT FACING TOTAL DOOM.
DARKSEID. HAS TO BE HIM. I CAN FEEL IT.
NEVER KNOW WHAT THEY'LL HIT US WITH...SHOULD THEY FIND US.
SHOULD HE FIND US. SHOULD DARKSEID FIND US. AND IF HE DOES...
...YOU CAN'T IMAGINE THE HORROR, CARRIE. YOU DON'T KNOW WHAT POWER IS.
I KNOW WHAT A BAD ATTITUDE IS, LARA.
AND I'M DAMNED SICK OF YOUR BAD ATTITUDE.
IF BIG OLD ROCK FACE COMES AT US, WE FIGHT BACK... WE COST HIM. MORE THAN HE CAN SPARE.
IT'S CALLED ATTRITION, SPACE GIRL. IT WORKS.
UNTIL THEN, WE HIDE?
LIKE LITTLE MICE?
LIKE RATS. THE KIND THAT CAN FLY.
THE KIND THAT CAN BITE, AND BITE DEEP.

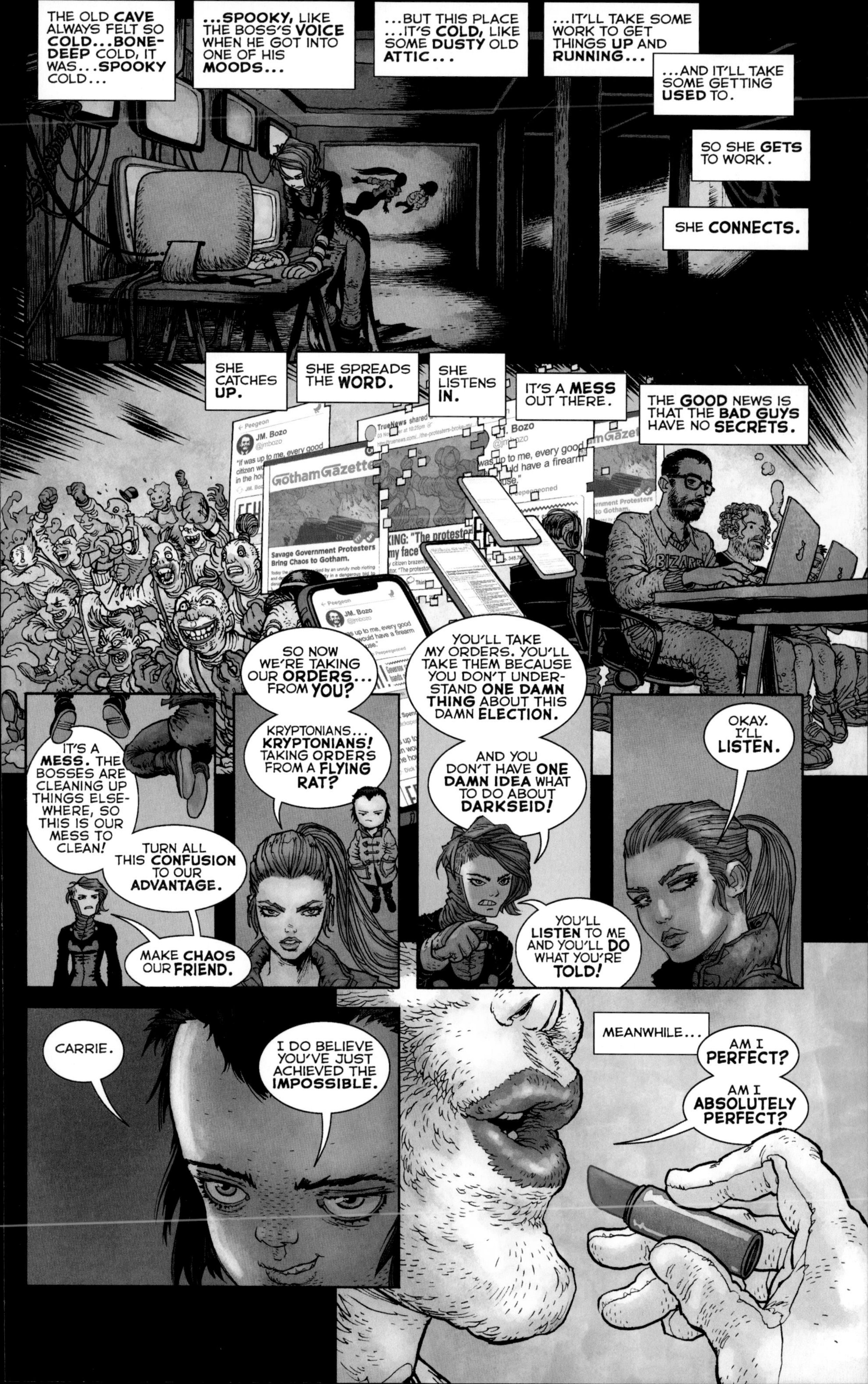
THE OLD CAVE ALWAYS FELT SO COLD...BONE-DEEP COLD, IT WAS...SPOOKY COLD...
...SPOOKY, LIKE THE BOSS'S VOICE WHEN HE GOT INTO ONE OF HIS MOODS...
...BUT THIS PLACE ...IT'S COLD, LIKE SOME DUSTY OLD ATTIC...
...IT'LL TAKE SOME WORK TO GET THINGS UP AND RUNNING...
...AND IT'LL TAKE SOME GETTING USED TO.
SO SHE GETS TO WORK.
SHE CONNECTS.
SHE CATCHES UP.
SHE SPREADS THE WORD.
SHE LISTENS IN.
IT'S A MESS OUT THERE.
THE GOOD NEWS IS THAT THE BAD GUYS HAVE NO SECRETS.
Gotham Gazette
Savage Government Protesters Bring Chaos to Gotham.
JM. Bozo
@jmbozo
"If was up to me, every good citizen would have a firearm in the house."
TrueNews shared
IT'S A MESS. THE BOSSES ARE CLEANING UP THINGS ELSE-WHERE, SO THIS IS OUR MESS TO CLEAN!
TURN ALL THIS CONFUSION TO OUR ADVANTAGE.
MAKE CHAOS OUR FRIEND.
SO NOW WE'RE TAKING OUR ORDERS... FROM YOU?
KRYPTONIANS... KRYPTONIANS! TAKING ORDERS FROM A FLYING RAT?
YOU'LL TAKE MY ORDERS. YOU'LL TAKE THEM BECAUSE YOU DON'T UNDER-STAND ONE DAMN THING ABOUT THIS DAMN ELECTION.
AND YOU DON'T HAVE ONE DAMN IDEA WHAT TO DO ABOUT DARKSEID!
YOU'LL LISTEN TO ME AND YOU'LL DO WHAT YOU'RE TOLD!
OKAY. I'LL LISTEN.
CARRIE.
I DO BELIEVE YOU'VE JUST ACHIEVED THE IMPOSSIBLE.
MEANWHILE...
AM I PERFECT?
AM I ABSOLUTELY PERFECT?

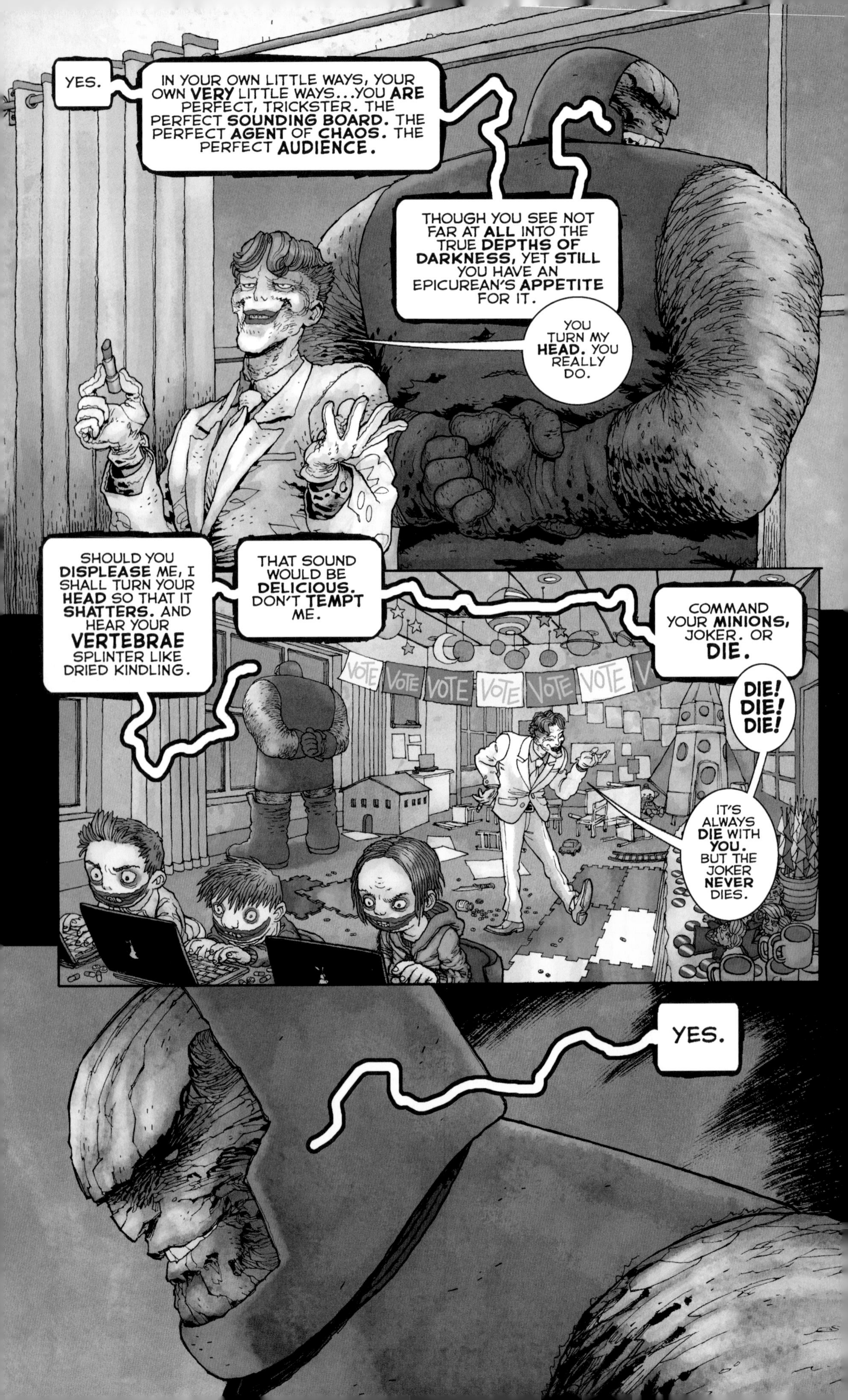
YES.
IN YOUR OWN LITTLE WAYS, YOUR OWN VERY LITTLE WAYS...YOU ARE PERFECT, TRICKSTER. THE PERFECT SOUNDING BOARD. THE PERFECT AGENT OF CHAOS. THE PERFECT AUDIENCE.
THOUGH YOU SEE NOT FAR AT ALL INTO THE TRUE DEPTHS OF DARKNESS, YET STILL YOU HAVE AN EPICUREAN'S APPETITE FOR IT.
YOU TURN MY HEAD. YOU REALLY DO.
SHOULD YOU DISPLEASE ME, I SHALL TURN YOUR HEAD SO THAT IT SHATTERS. AND HEAR YOUR VERTEBRAE SPLINTER LIKE DRIED KINDLING.
THAT SOUND WOULD BE DELICIOUS. DON'T TEMPT ME.
COMMAND YOUR MINIONS, JOKER. OR DIE.
VOTE VOTE VOTE VOTE VOTE VOTE
DIE! DIE! DIE!
IT'S ALWAYS DIE WITH YOU. BUT THE JOKER NEVER DIES.
YES.

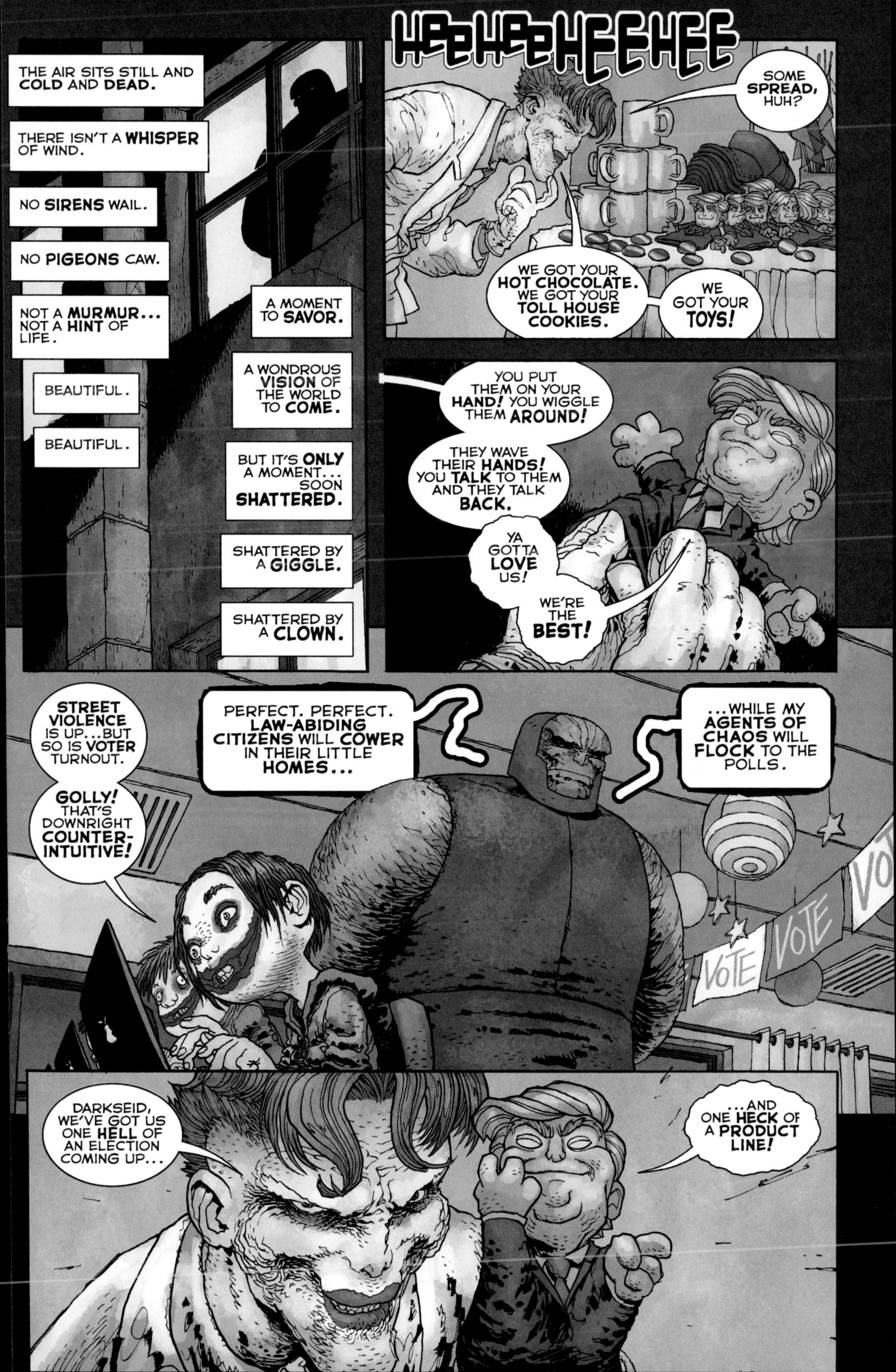
THE AIR SITS STILL AND COLD AND DEAD.
THERE ISN'T A WHISPER OF WIND.
NO SIRENS WAIL.
NO PIGEONS CAW.
NOT A MURMUR... NOT A HINT OF LIFE.
BEAUTIFUL.
BEAUTIFUL.
A MOMENT TO SAVOR.
A WONDROUS VISION OF THE WORLD TO COME.
BUT IT'S ONLY A MOMENT... SOON SHATTERED.
SHATTERED BY A GIGGLE.
SHATTERED BY A CLOWN.
HEE HEE HEE HEE
SOME SPREAD, HUH?
WE GOT YOUR HOT CHOCOLATE. WE GOT YOUR TOLL HOUSE COOKIES.
WE GOT YOUR TOYS!
YOU PUT THEM ON YOUR HAND! YOU WIGGLE THEM AROUND!
THEY WAVE THEIR HANDS! YOU TALK TO THEM AND THEY TALK BACK.
YA GOTTA LOVE US!
WE'RE THE BEST!
STREET VIOLENCE IS UP...BUT SO IS VOTER TURNOUT.
GOLLY! THAT'S DOWNRIGHT COUNTER-INTUITIVE!
PERFECT. PERFECT. LAW-ABIDING CITIZENS WILL COWER IN THEIR LITTLE HOMES...
...WHILE MY AGENTS OF CHAOS WILL FLOCK TO THE POLLS.
VOTE
VOTE
VOTE
DARKSEID, WE'VE GOT US ONE HELL OF AN ELECTION COMING UP...
...AND ONE HECK OF A PRODUCT LINE!

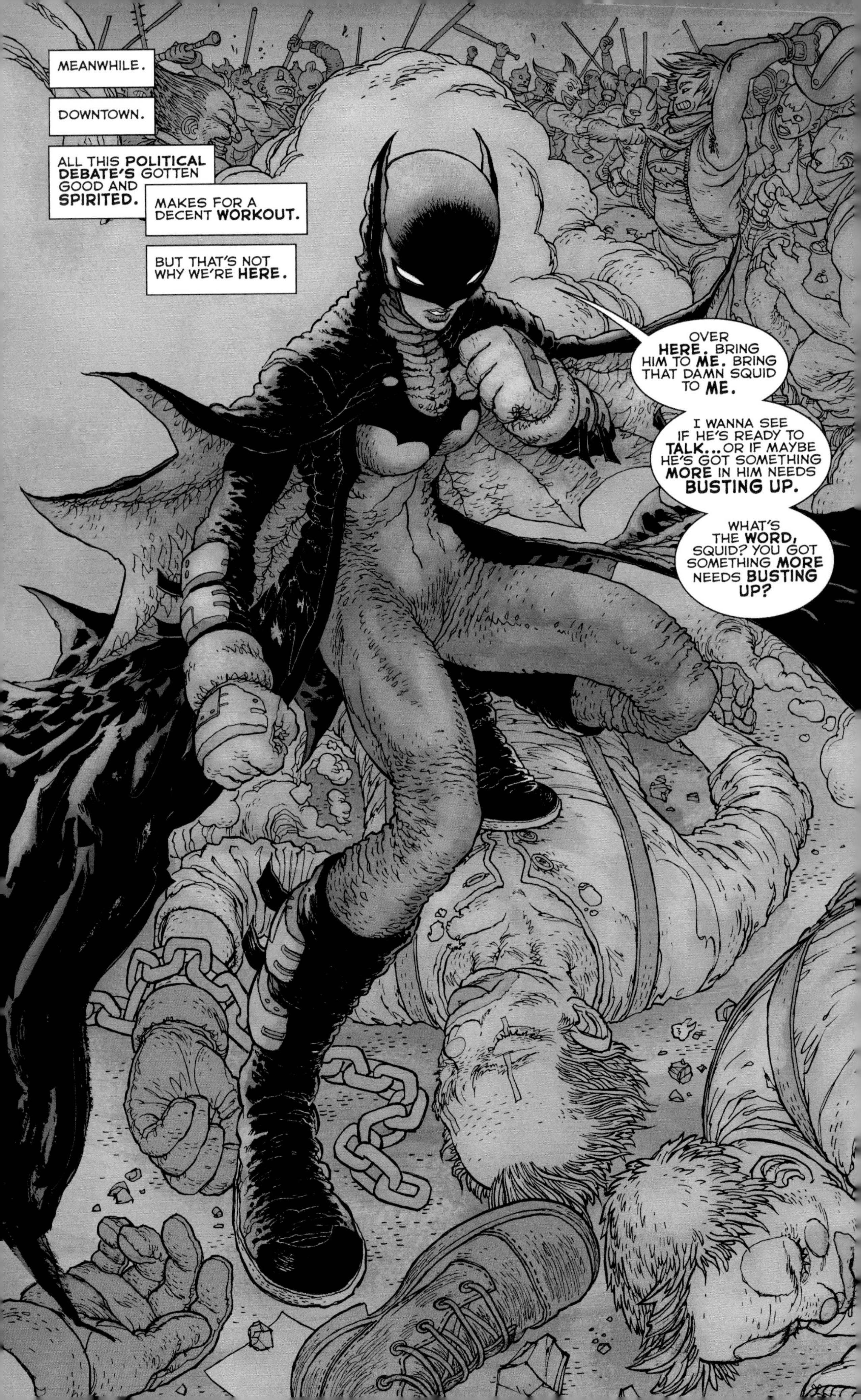
MEANWHILE.
DOWNTOWN.
ALL THIS POLITICAL DEBATE'S GOTTEN GOOD AND SPIRITED.
MAKES FOR A DECENT WORKOUT.
BUT THAT'S NOT WHY WE'RE HERE.
OVER HERE. BRING HIM TO ME. BRING THAT DAMN SQUID TO ME.
I WANNA SEE IF HE'S READY TO TALK...OR IF MAYBE HE'S GOT SOMETHING MORE IN HIM NEEDS BUSTING UP.
WHAT'S THE WORD, SQUID? YOU GOT SOMETHING MORE NEEDS BUSTING UP?

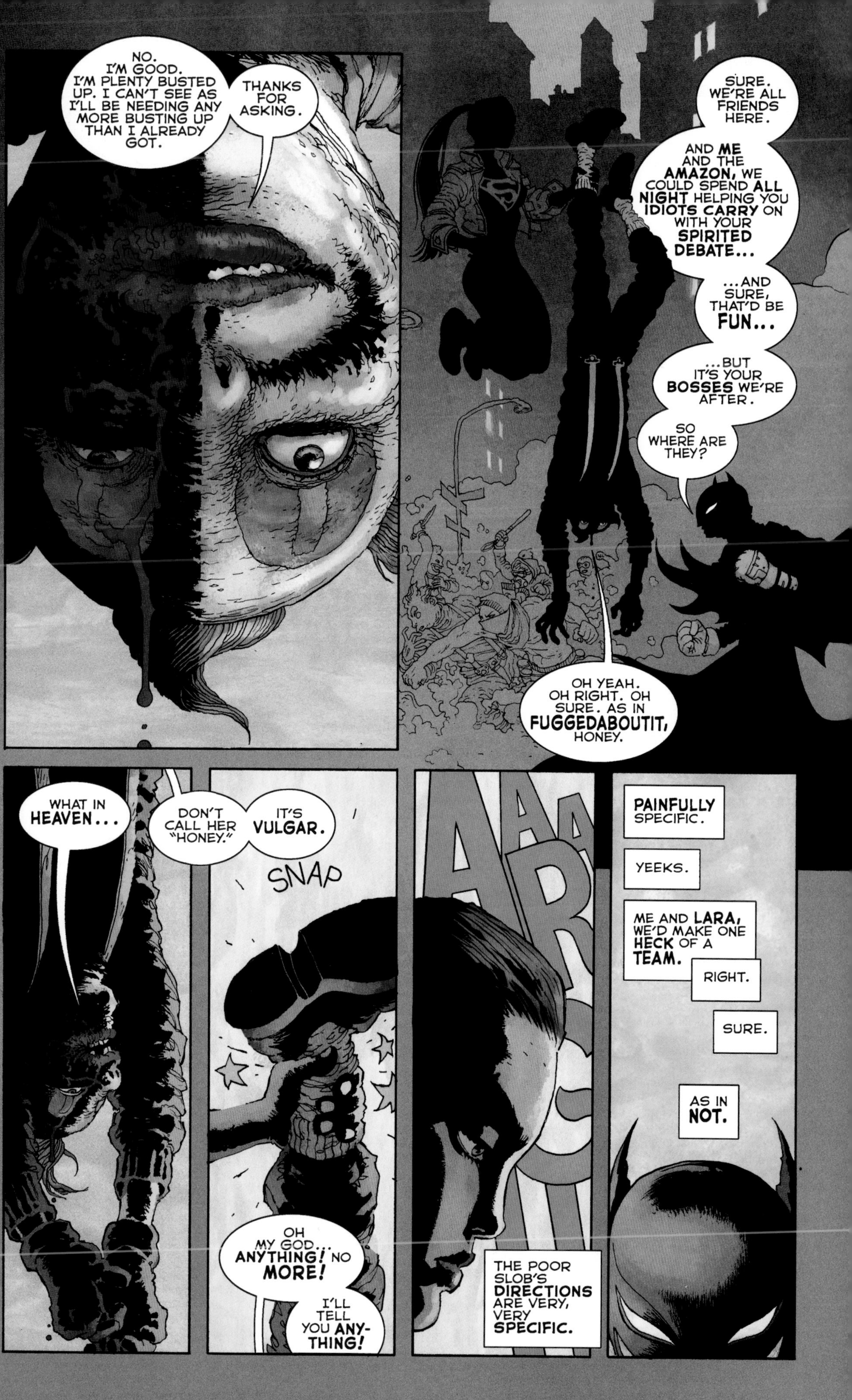
NO. I'M GOOD. I'M PLENTY BUSTED UP. I CAN'T SEE AS I'LL BE NEEDING ANY MORE BUSTING UP THAN I ALREADY GOT.
THANKS FOR ASKING.
SURE. WE'RE ALL FRIENDS HERE.
AND ME AND THE AMAZON, WE COULD SPEND ALL NIGHT HELPING YOU IDIOTS CARRY ON WITH YOUR SPIRITED DEBATE...
...AND SURE, THAT'D BE FUN...
...BUT IT'S YOUR BOSSES WE'RE AFTER.
SO WHERE ARE THEY?
OH YEAH. OH RIGHT. OH SURE. AS IN FUGGEDABOUTIT, HONEY.
WHAT IN HEAVEN...
DON'T CALL HER "HONEY."
IT'S VULGAR.
SNAP
OH MY GOD... ANYTHING! NO MORE!
I'LL TELL YOU ANYTHING!
AAAARR
THE POOR SLOB'S DIRECTIONS ARE VERY, VERY SPECIFIC.
PAINFULLY SPECIFIC.
YEEKS.
ME AND LARA, WE'D MAKE ONE HECK OF A TEAM.
RIGHT.
SURE.
AS IN NOT.

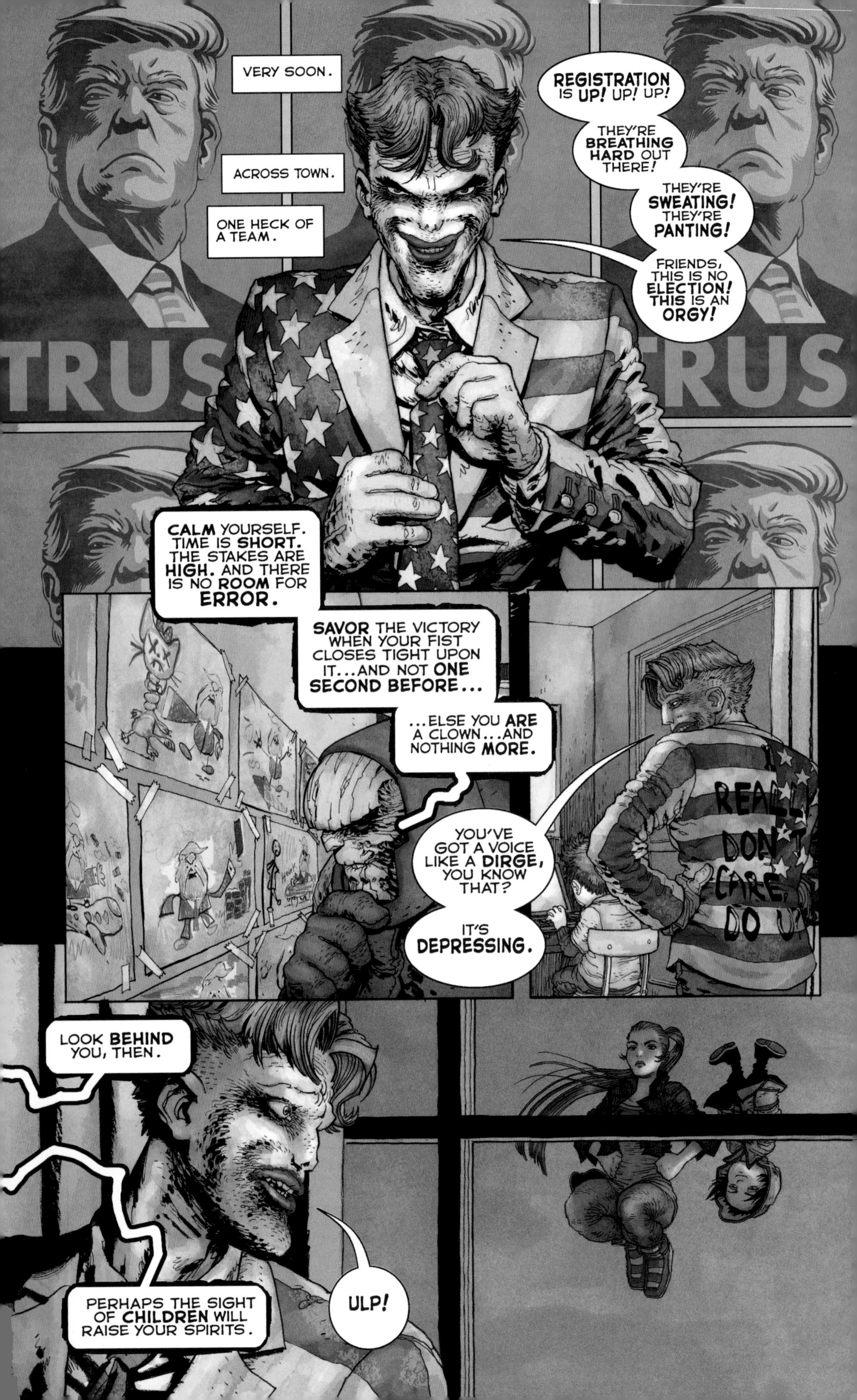
VERY SOON.
ACROSS TOWN.
ONE HECK OF A TEAM.
REGISTRATION IS UP! UP! UP!
THEY'RE BREATHING HARD OUT THERE!
THEY'RE SWEATING! THEY'RE PANTING!
FRIENDS, THIS IS NO ELECTION! THIS IS AN ORGY!
TRUS
TRUS
CALM YOURSELF. TIME IS SHORT. THE STAKES ARE HIGH. AND THERE IS NO ROOM FOR ERROR.
SAVOR THE VICTORY WHEN YOUR FIST CLOSES TIGHT UPON IT...AND NOT ONE SECOND BEFORE...
...ELSE YOU ARE A CLOWN...AND NOTHING MORE.
YOU'VE GOT A VOICE LIKE A DIRGE, YOU KNOW THAT?
IT'S DEPRESSING.
LOOK BEHIND YOU, THEN.
PERHAPS THE SIGHT OF CHILDREN WILL RAISE YOUR SPIRITS.
ULP!

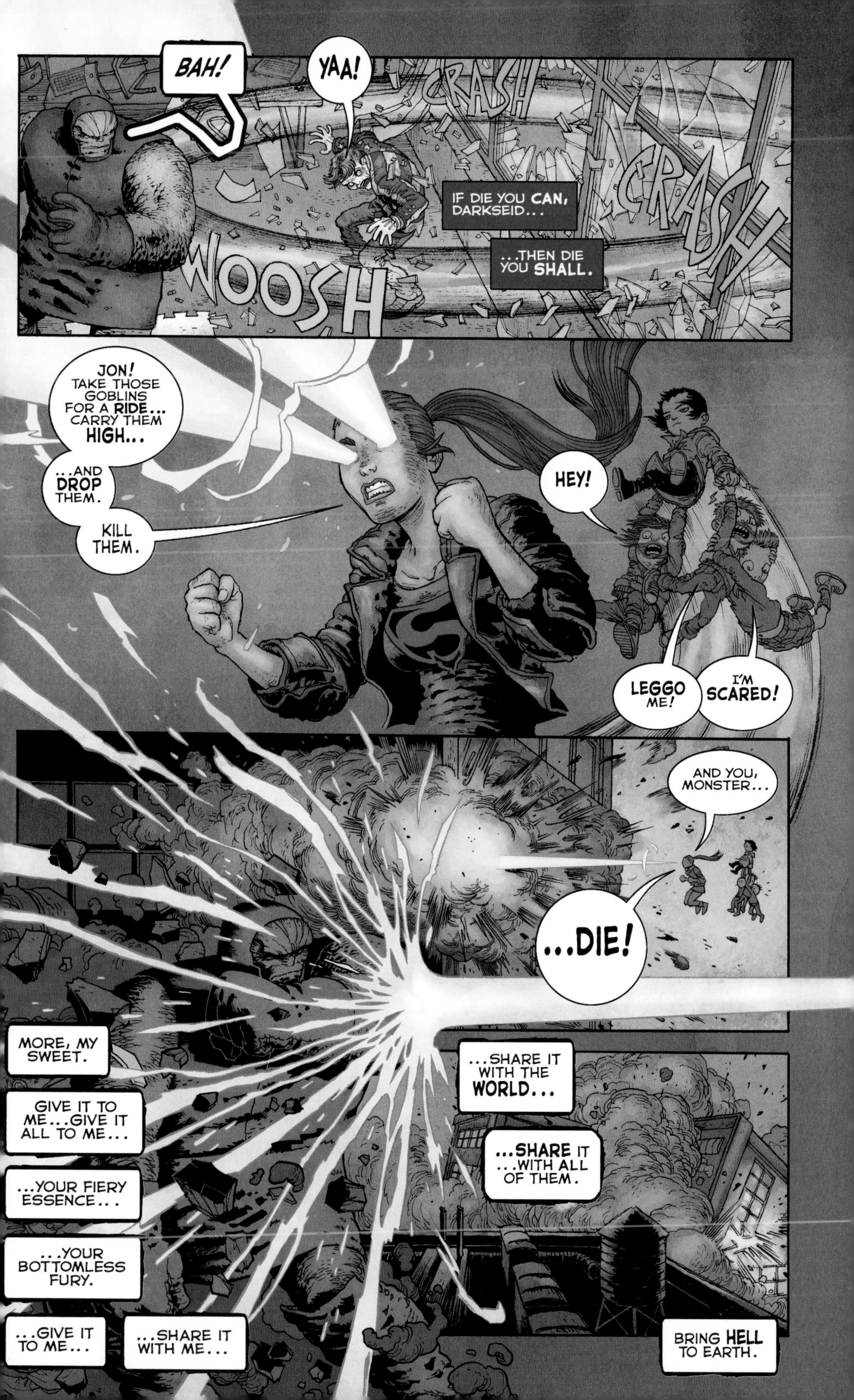
BAH!
YAA!
CRASH
CRASH
IF DIE YOU CAN, DARKSEID...
...THEN DIE YOU SHALL.
WOOSH
JON! TAKE THOSE GOBLINS FOR A RIDE... CARRY THEM HIGH...
...AND DROP THEM.
KILL THEM.
HEY!
LEGGO ME!
I'M SCARED!
AND YOU, MONSTER...
...DIE!
MORE, MY SWEET.
GIVE IT TO ME...GIVE IT ALL TO ME...
...YOUR FIERY ESSENCE...
...YOUR BOTTOMLESS FURY.
...GIVE IT TO ME...
...SHARE IT WITH ME...
...SHARE IT WITH THE WORLD...
...SHARE IT ...WITH ALL OF THEM.
BRING HELL TO EARTH.

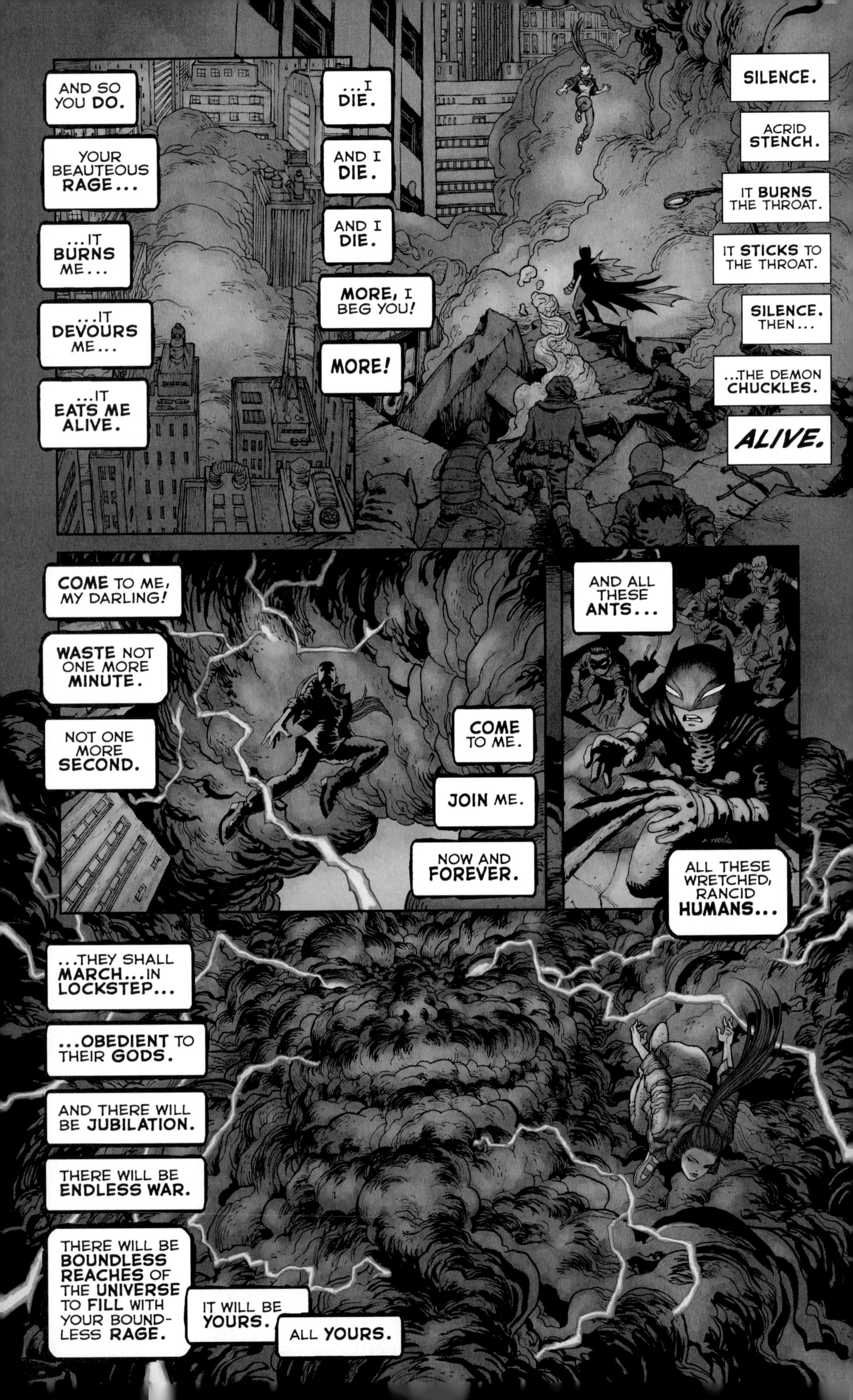
AND SO YOU DO.
YOUR BEAUTEOUS RAGE...
...IT BURNS ME...
...IT DEVOURS ME...
...IT EATS ME ALIVE.
...I DIE.
AND I DIE.
AND I DIE.
MORE, I BEG YOU!
MORE!
SILENCE.
ACRID STENCH.
IT BURNS THE THROAT.
IT STICKS TO THE THROAT.
SILENCE. THEN...
...THE DEMON CHUCKLES.
ALIVE.
COME TO ME, MY DARLING!
WASTE NOT ONE MORE MINUTE.
NOT ONE MORE SECOND.
COME TO ME.
JOIN ME.
NOW AND FOREVER.
AND ALL THESE ANTS...
ALL THESE WRETCHED, RANCID HUMANS...
...THEY SHALL MARCH...IN LOCKSTEP...
...OBEDIENT TO THEIR GODS.
AND THERE WILL BE JUBILATION.
THERE WILL BE ENDLESS WAR.
THERE WILL BE BOUNDLESS REACHES OF THE UNIVERSE TO FILL WITH YOUR BOUNDLESS RAGE.
IT WILL BE YOURS.
ALL YOURS.

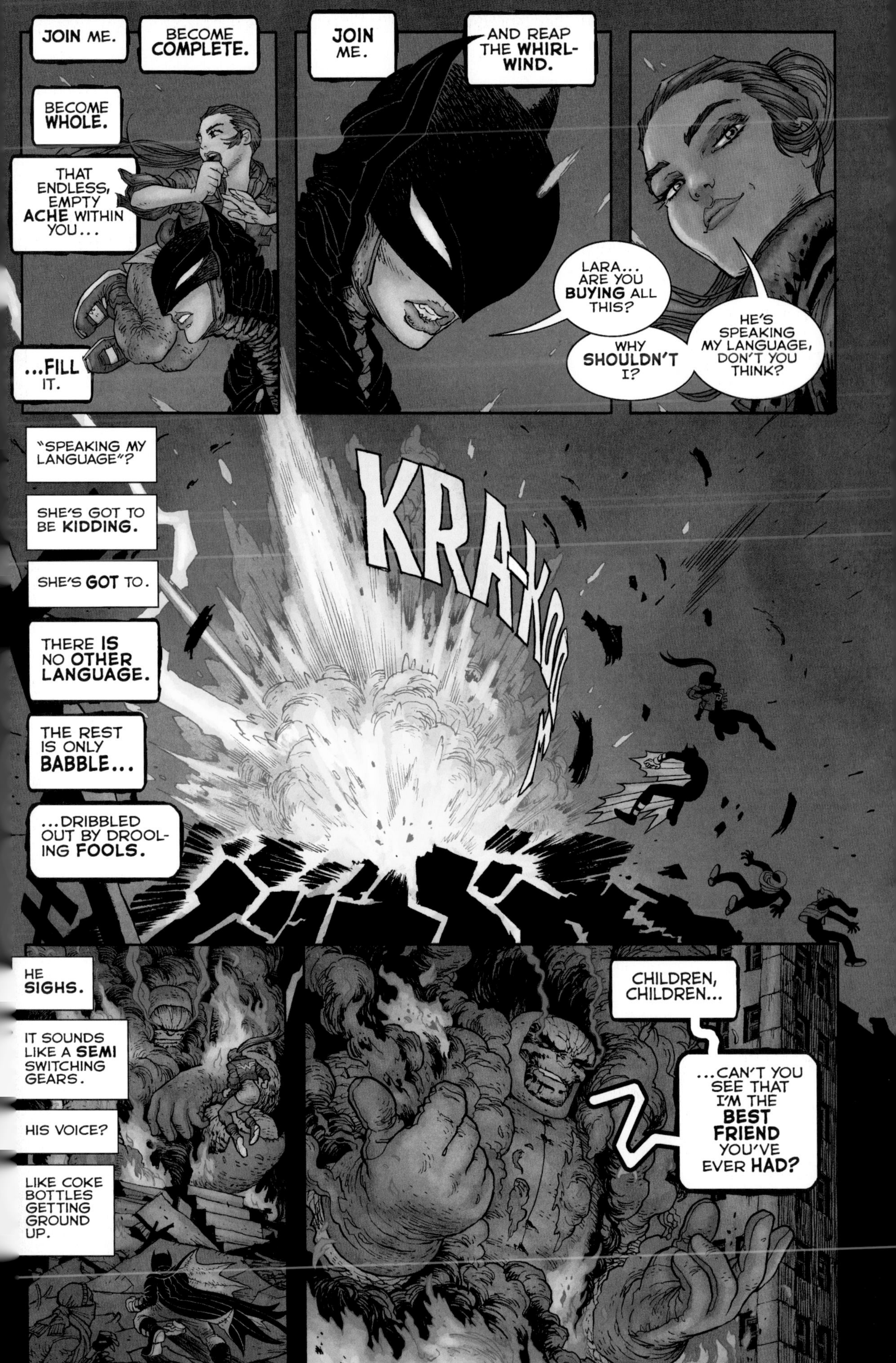

JOIN ME.
BECOME COMPLETE.
BECOME WHOLE.
THAT ENDLESS, EMPTY ACHE WITHIN YOU...
...FILL IT.
JOIN ME.
AND REAP THE WHIRL-WIND.
LARA... ARE YOU BUYING ALL THIS?
WHY SHOULDN'T I?
HE'S SPEAKING MY LANGUAGE, DON'T YOU THINK?
"SPEAKING MY LANGUAGE"?
SHE'S GOT TO BE KIDDING.
SHE'S GOT TO.
THERE IS NO OTHER LANGUAGE.
THE REST IS ONLY BABBLE...
...DRIBBLED OUT BY DROOL-ING FOOLS.
KRA-KOOM
HE SIGHS.
IT SOUNDS LIKE A SEMI SWITCHING GEARS.
HIS VOICE?
LIKE COKE BOTTLES GETTING GROUND UP.
CHILDREN, CHILDREN...
...CAN'T YOU SEE THAT I'M THE BEST FRIEND YOU'VE EVER HAD?

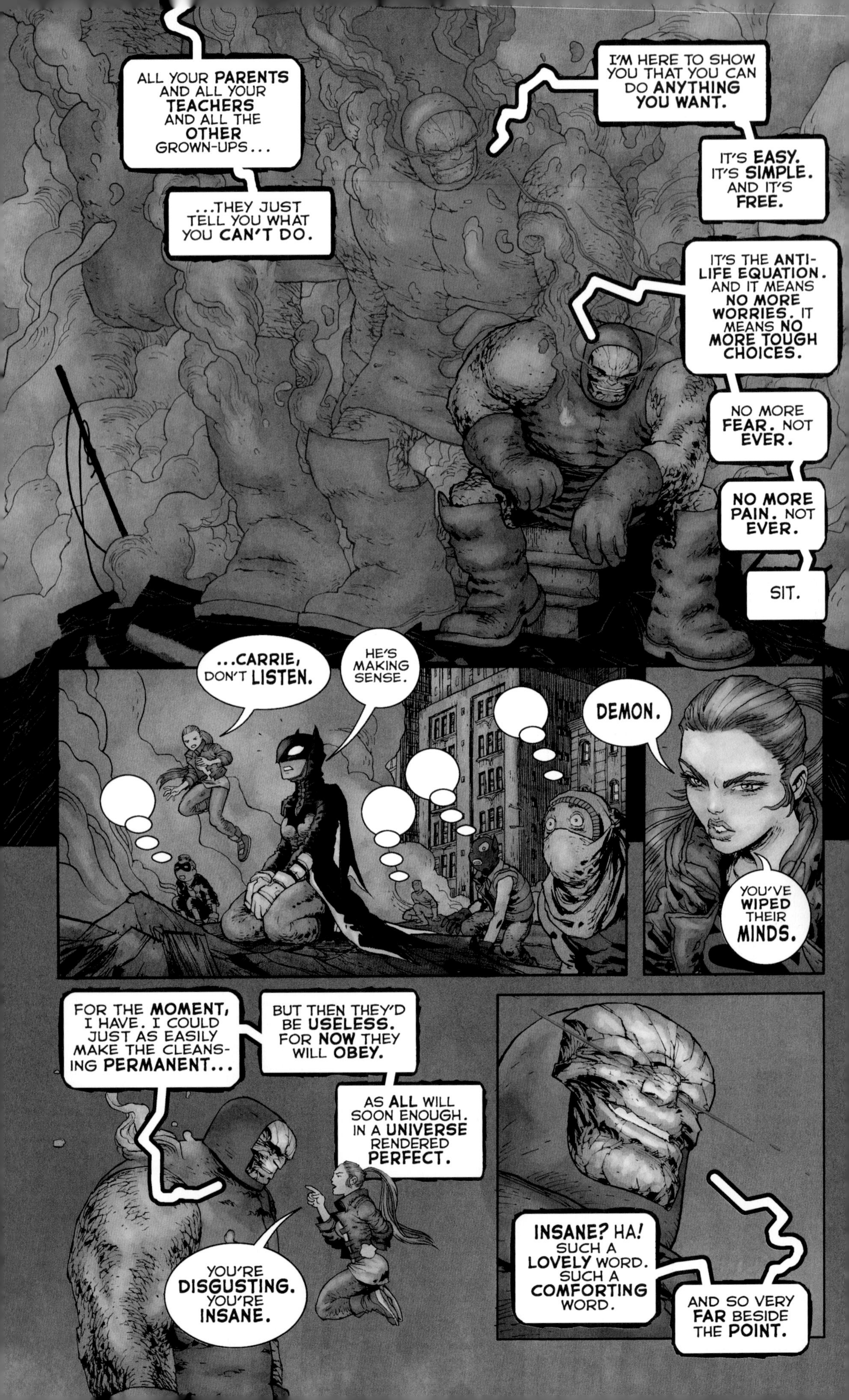
ALL YOUR PARENTS AND ALL YOUR TEACHERS AND ALL THE OTHER GROWN-UPS...
...THEY JUST TELL YOU WHAT YOU CAN'T DO.
I'M HERE TO SHOW YOU THAT YOU CAN DO ANYTHING YOU WANT.
IT'S EASY. IT'S SIMPLE. AND IT'S FREE.
IT'S THE ANTI-LIFE EQUATION. AND IT MEANS NO MORE WORRIES. IT MEANS NO MORE TOUGH CHOICES.
NO MORE FEAR. NOT EVER.
NO MORE PAIN. NOT EVER.
SIT.
...CARRIE, DON'T LISTEN.
HE'S MAKING SENSE.
DEMON.
YOU'VE WIPED THEIR MINDS.
FOR THE MOMENT, I HAVE. I COULD JUST AS EASILY MAKE THE CLEANSING PERMANENT...
BUT THEN THEY'D BE USELESS. FOR NOW THEY WILL OBEY.
AS ALL WILL SOON ENOUGH. IN A UNIVERSE RENDERED PERFECT.
YOU'RE DISGUSTING. YOU'RE INSANE.
INSANE? HA! SUCH A LOVELY WORD. SUCH A COMFORTING WORD.
AND SO VERY FAR BESIDE THE POINT.

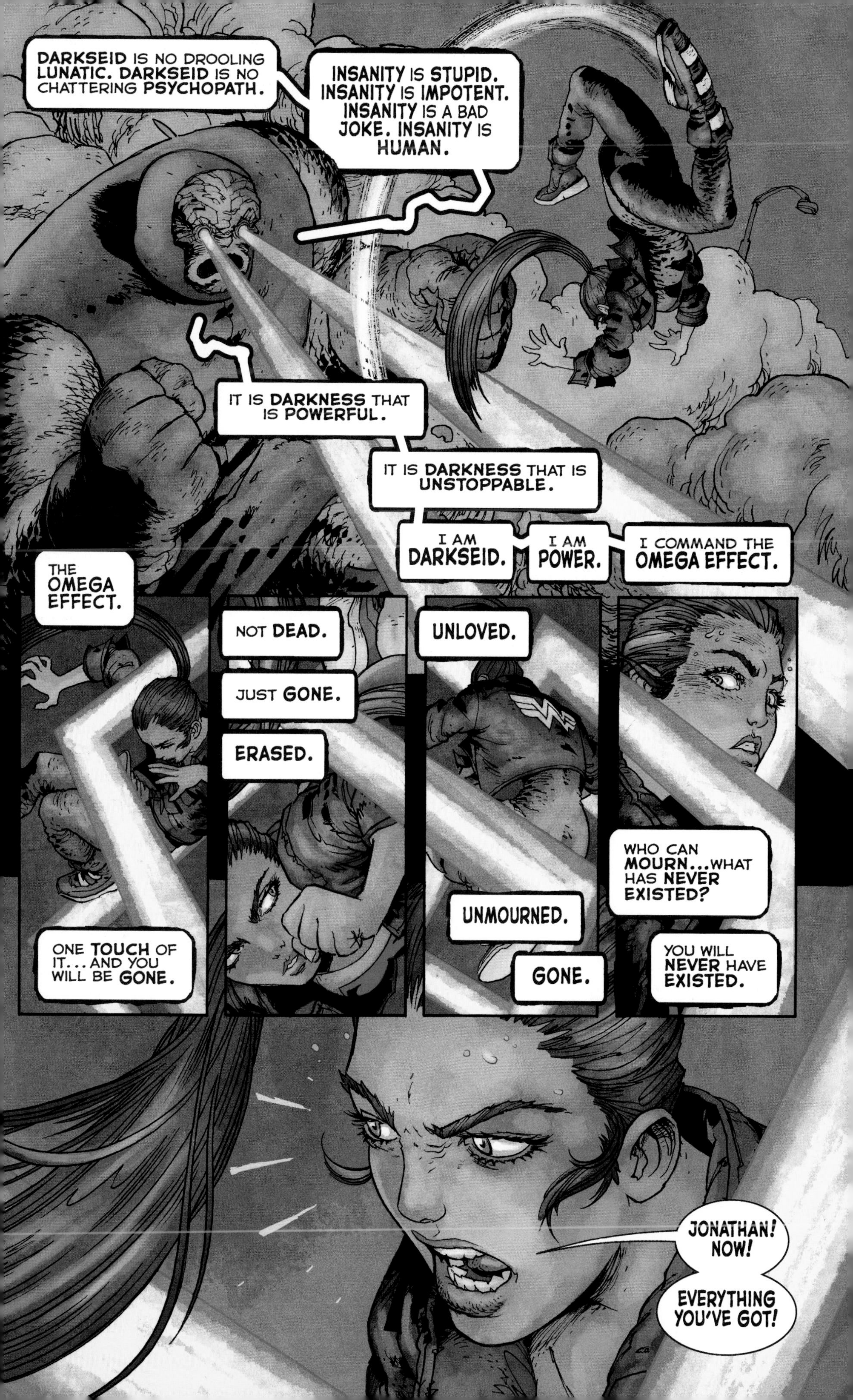
DARKSEID IS NO DROOLING LUNATIC. DARKSEID IS NO CHATTERING PSYCHOPATH.
INSANITY IS STUPID. INSANITY IS IMPOTENT. INSANITY IS A BAD JOKE. INSANITY IS HUMAN.
IT IS DARKNESS THAT IS POWERFUL.
IT IS DARKNESS THAT IS UNSTOPPABLE.
I AM DARKSEID.
I AM POWER.
I COMMAND THE OMEGA EFFECT.
THE OMEGA EFFECT.
ONE TOUCH OF IT... AND YOU WILL BE GONE.
NOT DEAD.
JUST GONE.
ERASED.
UNLOVED.
UNMOURNED.
GONE.
WHO CAN MOURN...WHAT HAS NEVER EXISTED?
YOU WILL NEVER HAVE EXISTED.
JONATHAN! NOW!
EVERYTHING YOU'VE GOT!

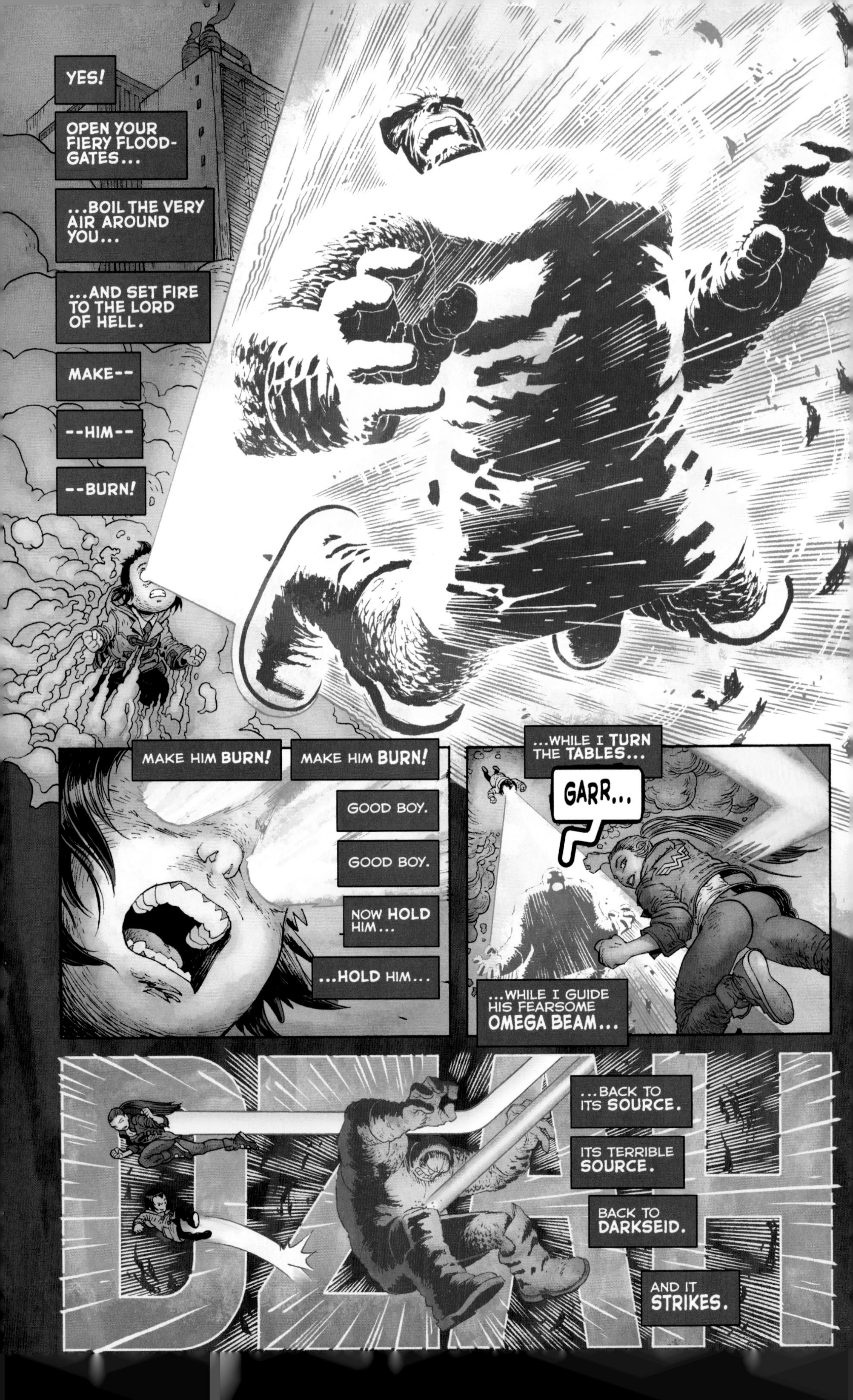
YES!
OPEN YOUR FIERY FLOOD-GATES...
...BOIL THE VERY AIR AROUND YOU...
...AND SET FIRE TO THE LORD OF HELL.
MAKE--
--HIM--
--BURN!
MAKE HIM BURN!
MAKE HIM BURN!
GOOD BOY.
GOOD BOY.
NOW HOLD HIM...
...HOLD HIM...
...WHILE I TURN THE TABLES...
GARR...
...WHILE I GUIDE HIS FEARSOME OMEGA BEAM...
...BACK TO ITS SOURCE.
ITS TERRIBLE SOURCE.
BACK TO DARKSEID.
AND IT STRIKES.

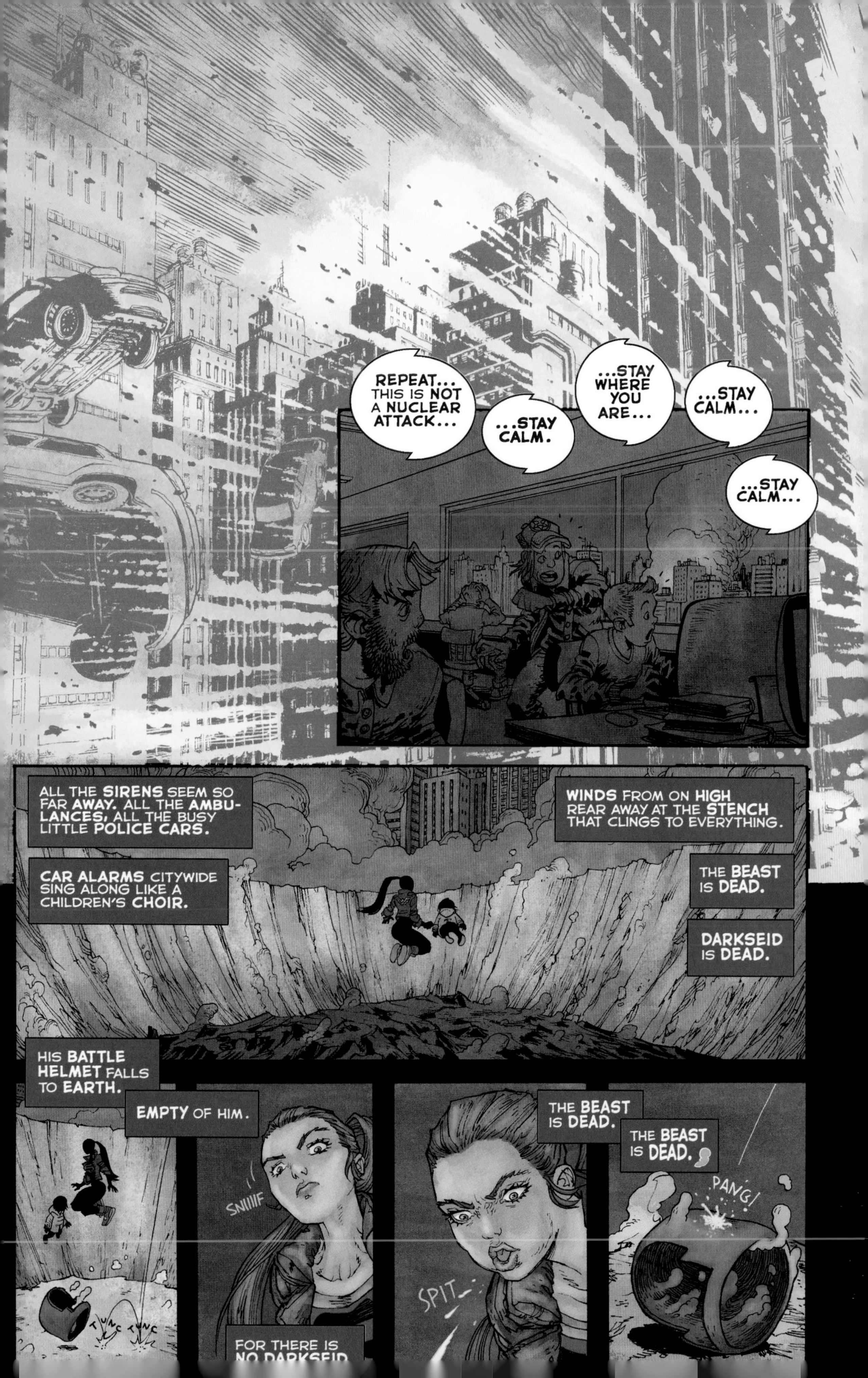
REPEAT... THIS IS NOT A NUCLEAR ATTACK...
...STAY CALM.
...STAY WHERE YOU ARE...
...STAY CALM...
...STAY CALM...
ALL THE SIRENS SEEM SO FAR AWAY. ALL THE AMBULANCES, ALL THE BUSY LITTLE POLICE CARS.
CAR ALARMS CITYWIDE SING ALONG LIKE A CHILDREN'S CHOIR.
WINDS FROM ON HIGH REAR AWAY AT THE STENCH THAT CLINGS TO EVERYTHING.
THE BEAST IS DEAD.
DARKSEID IS DEAD.
HIS BATTLE HELMET FALLS TO EARTH.
EMPTY OF HIM.
TUNC TUNC
SNIIIIF
FOR THERE IS NO DARKSEID
THE BEAST IS DEAD.
THE BEAST IS DEAD.
SPIT
PANG!

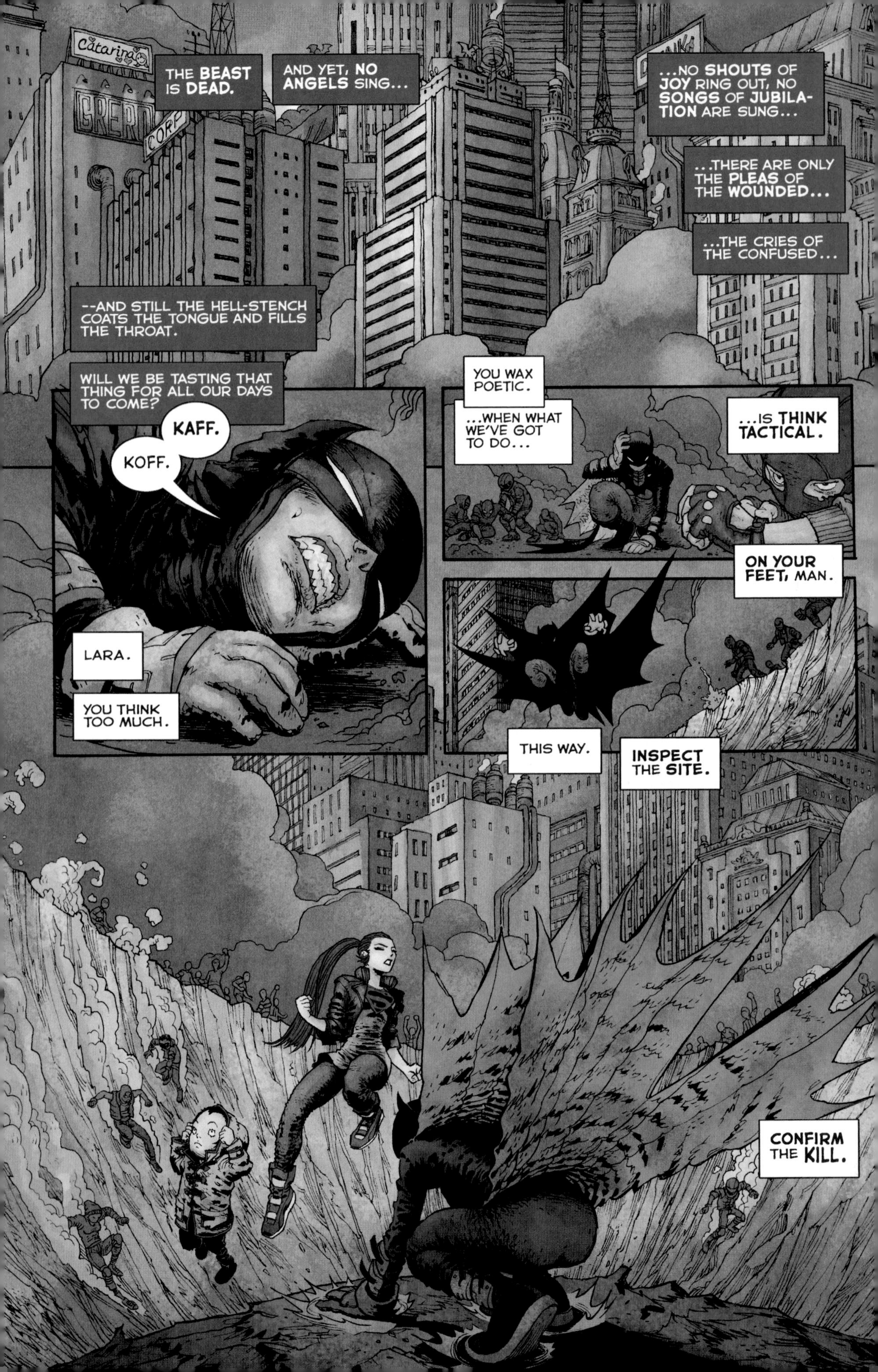
THE BEAST IS DEAD.
AND YET, NO ANGELS SING...
...NO SHOUTS OF JOY RING OUT, NO SONGS OF JUBILA-TION ARE SUNG...
...THERE ARE ONLY THE PLEAS OF THE WOUNDED...
...THE CRIES OF THE CONFUSED...
--AND STILL THE HELL-STENCH COATS THE TONGUE AND FILLS THE THROAT.
WILL WE BE TASTING THAT THING FOR ALL OUR DAYS TO COME?
KAFF.
KOFF.
LARA.
YOU THINK TOO MUCH.
YOU WAX POETIC.
...WHEN WHAT WE'VE GOT TO DO...
...IS THINK TACTICAL.
ON YOUR FEET, MAN.
THIS WAY.
INSPECT THE SITE.
CONFIRM THE KILL.

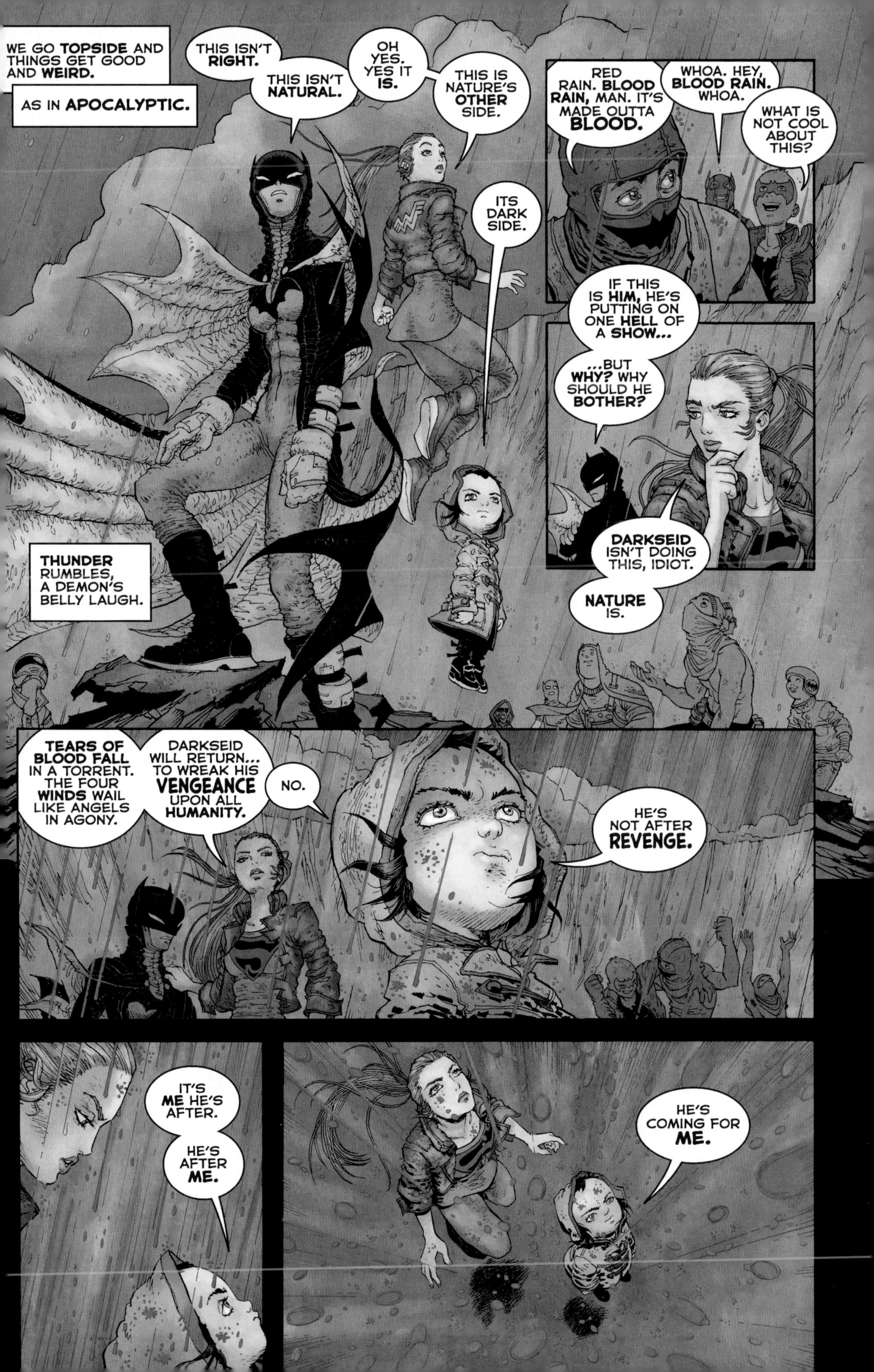

WE GO TOPSIDE AND THINGS GET GOOD AND WEIRD.
AS IN APOCALYPTIC.
THIS ISN'T RIGHT.
THIS ISN'T NATURAL.
OH YES. YES IT IS.
THIS IS NATURE'S OTHER SIDE.
ITS DARK SIDE.
RED RAIN. BLOOD RAIN, MAN. IT'S MADE OUTTA BLOOD.
WHOA. HEY, BLOOD RAIN. WHOA.
WHAT IS NOT COOL ABOUT THIS?
IF THIS IS HIM, HE'S PUTTING ON ONE HELL OF A SHOW...
...BUT WHY? WHY SHOULD HE BOTHER?
DARKSEID ISN'T DOING THIS, IDIOT.
NATURE IS.
THUNDER RUMBLES, A DEMON'S BELLY LAUGH.
TEARS OF BLOOD FALL IN A TORRENT. THE FOUR WINDS WAIL LIKE ANGELS IN AGONY.
DARKSEID WILL RETURN... TO WREAK HIS VENGEANCE UPON ALL HUMANITY.
NO.
HE'S NOT AFTER REVENGE.
IT'S ME HE'S AFTER.
HE'S AFTER ME.
HE'S COMING FOR ME.

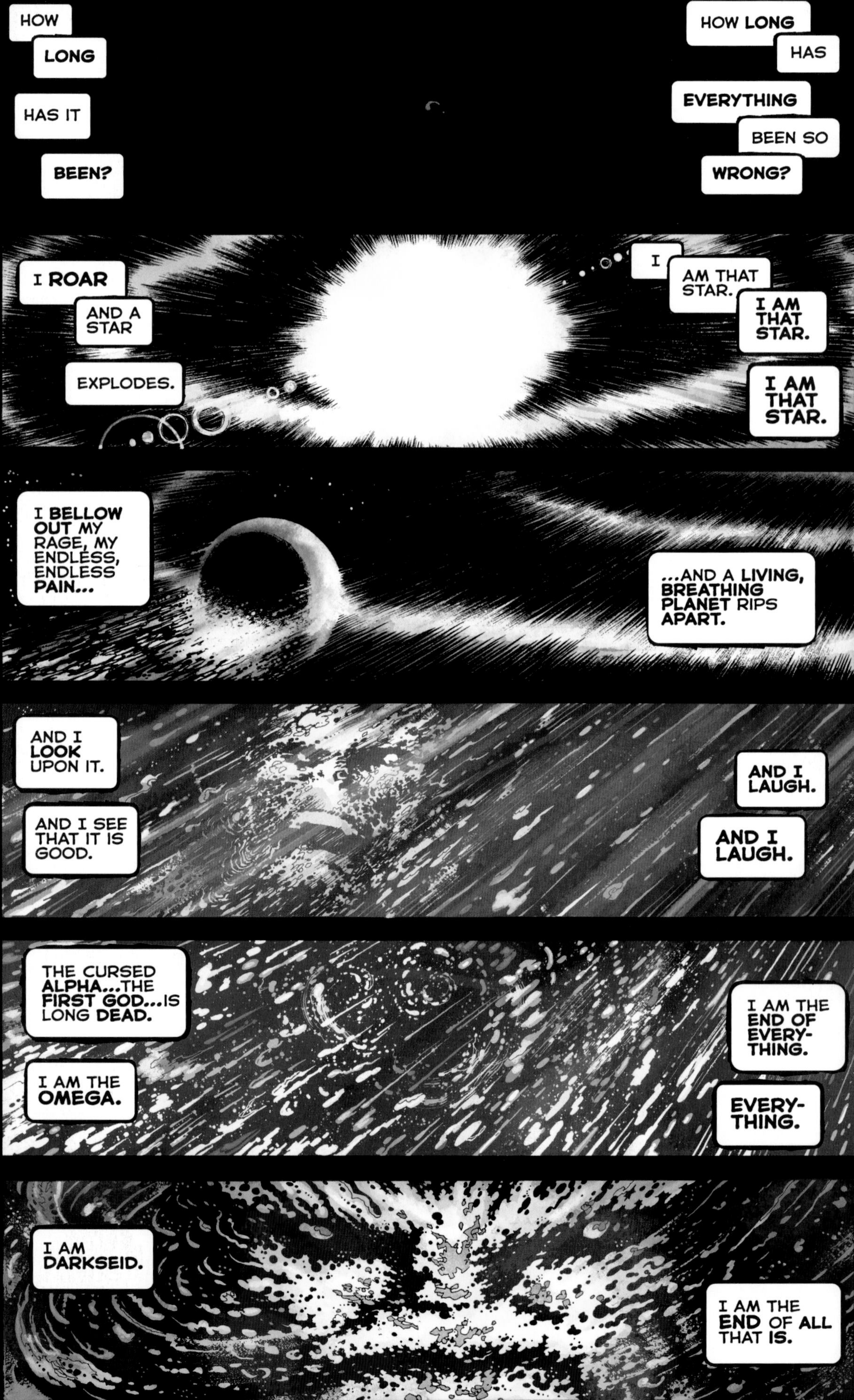
HOW
LONG
HAS IT
BEEN?
HOW LONG
HAS
EVERYTHING
BEEN SO
WRONG?
I ROAR
AND A STAR
EXPLODES.
I
AM THAT STAR.
I AM THAT STAR.
I AM THAT STAR.
I BELLOW OUT MY RAGE, MY ENDLESS, ENDLESS PAIN...
...AND A LIVING, BREATHING PLANET RIPS APART.
AND I LOOK UPON IT.
AND I SEE THAT IT IS GOOD.
AND I LAUGH.
AND I LAUGH.
THE CURSED ALPHA...THE FIRST GOD...IS LONG DEAD.
I AM THE OMEGA.
I AM THE END OF EVERY-THING.
EVERY-THING.
I AM DARKSEID.
I AM THE END OF ALL THAT IS.

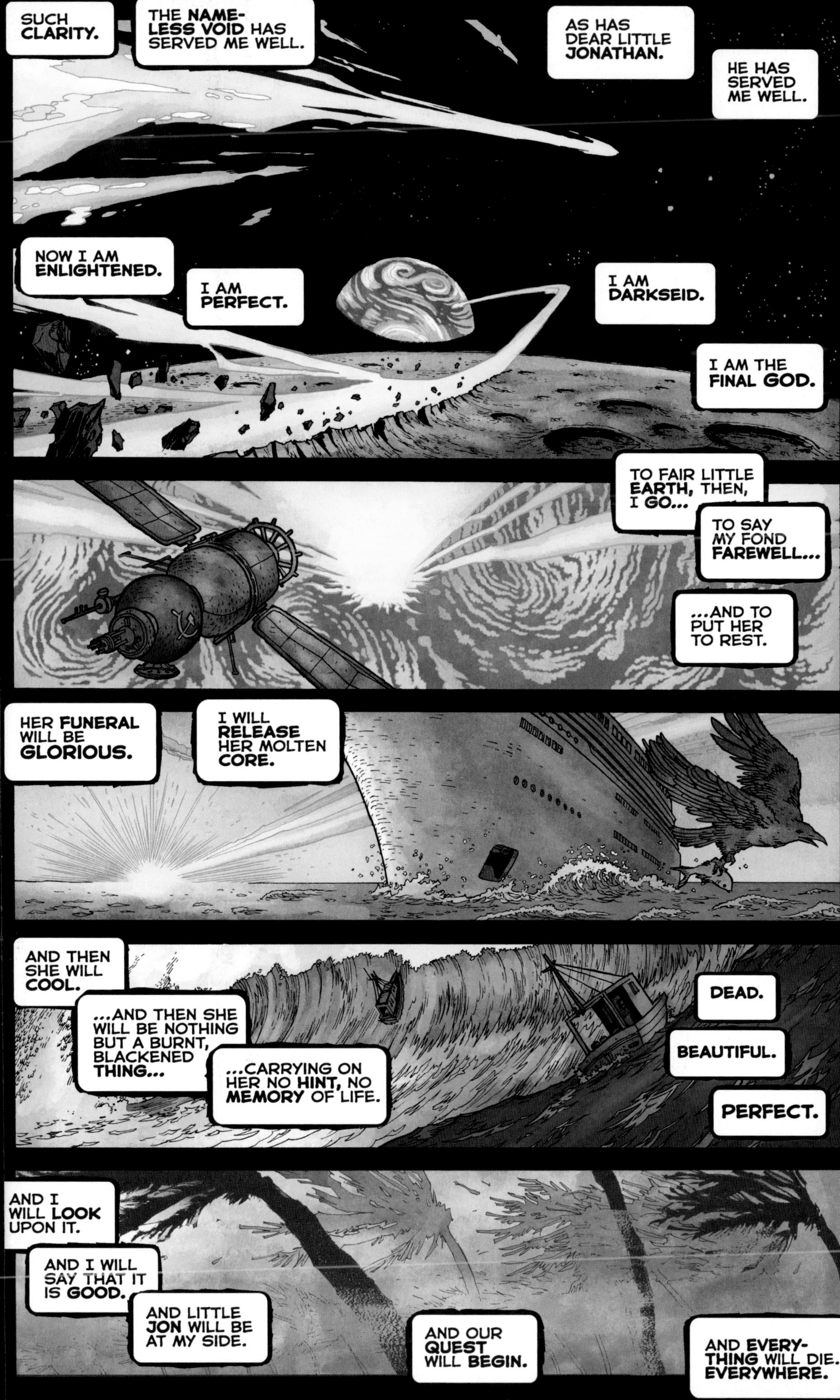

SUCH CLARITY.
THE NAMELESS VOID HAS SERVED ME WELL.
AS HAS DEAR LITTLE JONATHAN.
HE HAS SERVED ME WELL.
NOW I AM ENLIGHTENED.
I AM PERFECT.
I AM DARKSEID.
I AM THE FINAL GOD.
TO FAIR LITTLE EARTH, THEN, I GO...
TO SAY MY FOND FAREWELL...
...AND TO PUT HER TO REST.
HER FUNERAL WILL BE GLORIOUS.
I WILL RELEASE HER MOLTEN CORE.
AND THEN SHE WILL COOL.
...AND THEN SHE WILL BE NOTHING BUT A BURNT, BLACKENED THING...
...CARRYING ON HER NO HINT, NO MEMORY OF LIFE.
DEAD.
BEAUTIFUL.
PERFECT.
AND I WILL LOOK UPON IT.
AND I WILL SAY THAT IT IS GOOD.
AND LITTLE JON WILL BE AT MY SIDE.
AND OUR QUEST WILL BEGIN.
AND EVERYTHING WILL DIE. EVERYWHERE.

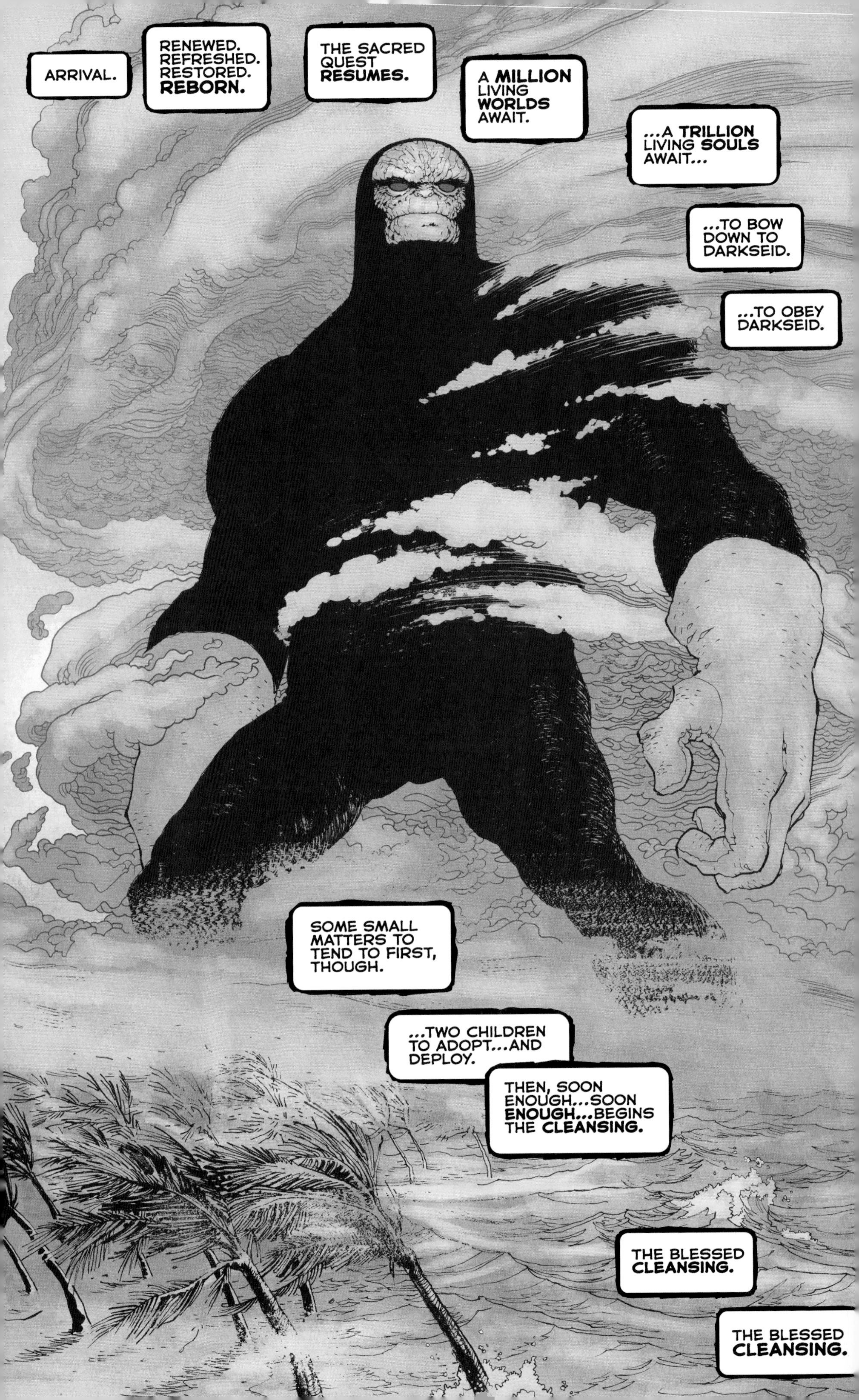

ARRIVAL.
RENEWED. REFRESHED. RESTORED. REBORN.
THE SACRED QUEST RESUMES.
A MILLION LIVING WORLDS AWAIT.
...A TRILLION LIVING SOULS AWAIT...
...TO BOW DOWN TO DARKSEID.
...TO OBEY DARKSEID.
SOME SMALL MATTERS TO TEND TO FIRST, THOUGH.
...TWO CHILDREN TO ADOPT...AND DEPLOY.
THEN, SOON ENOUGH...SOON ENOUGH...BEGINS THE CLEANSING.
THE BLESSED CLEANSING.
THE BLESSED CLEANSING.

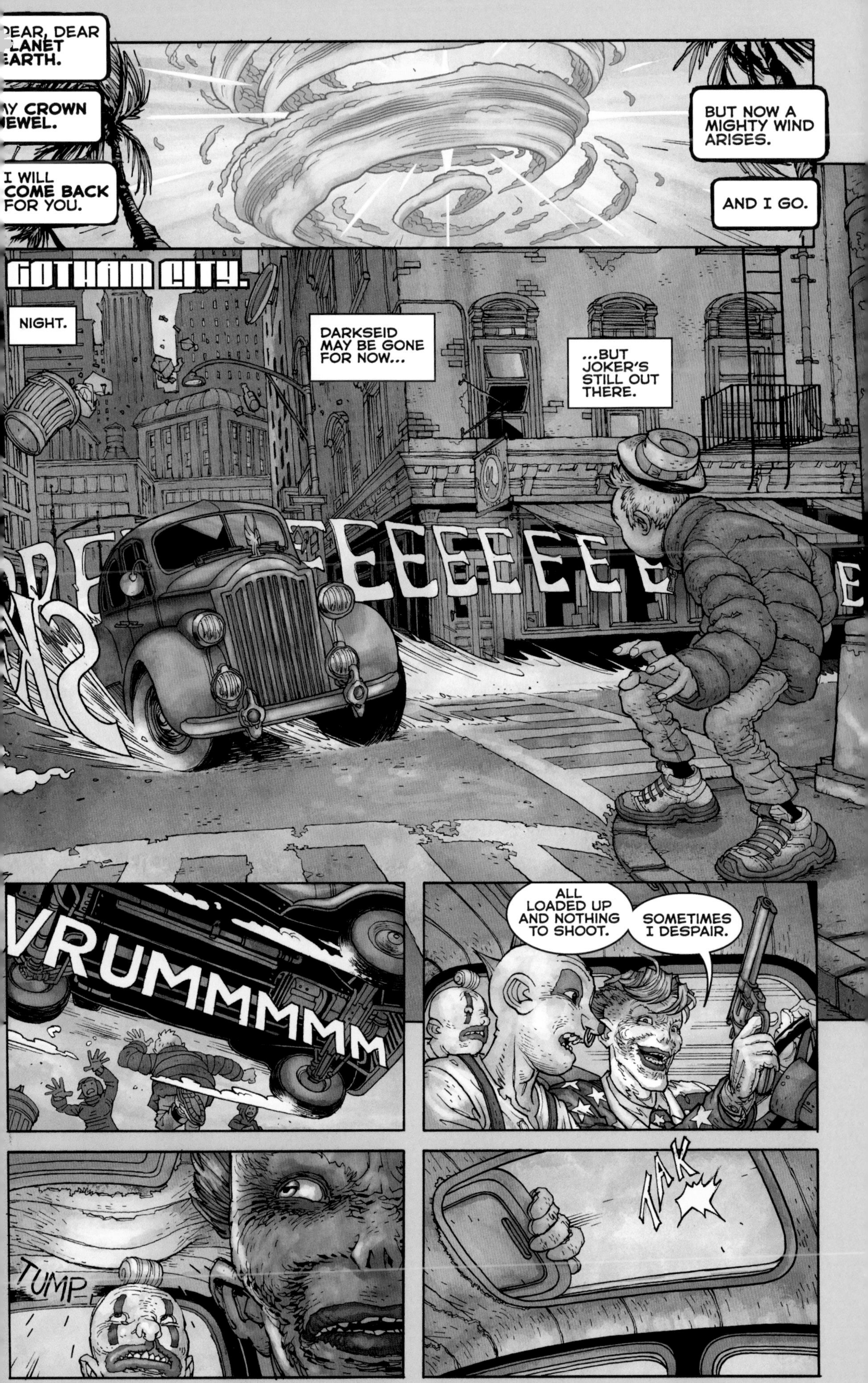

DEAR, DEAR PLANET EARTH.
MY CROWN JEWEL.
I WILL COME BACK FOR YOU.
BUT NOW A MIGHTY WIND ARISES.
AND I GO.
GOTHAM CITY.
NIGHT.
DARKSEID MAY BE GONE FOR NOW...
...BUT JOKER'S STILL OUT THERE.
EEEEEEE
VRUMMMMMM
ALL LOADED UP AND NOTHING TO SHOOT.
SOMETIMES I DESPAIR.
TUMP
TAK

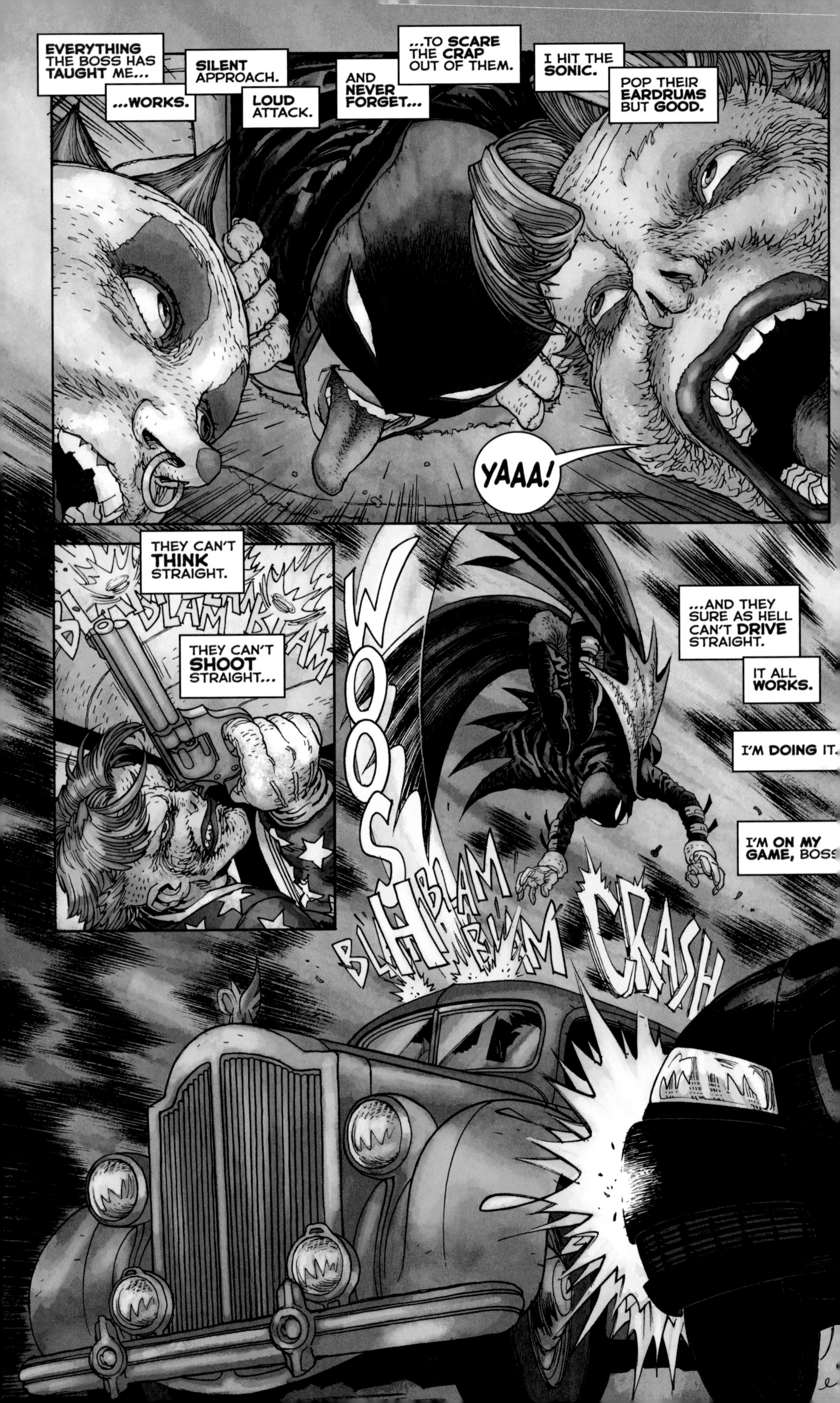
EVERYTHING THE BOSS HAS TAUGHT ME...
...WORKS.
SILENT APPROACH.
LOUD ATTACK.
AND NEVER FORGET...
...TO SCARE THE CRAP OUT OF THEM.
I HIT THE SONIC.
POP THEIR EARDRUMS BUT GOOD.
YAAA!
THEY CAN'T THINK STRAIGHT.
BLAM
BLAM
THEY CAN'T SHOOT STRAIGHT...
WOOOSH
...AND THEY SURE AS HELL CAN'T DRIVE STRAIGHT.
IT ALL WORKS.
I'M DOING IT.
I'M ON MY GAME, BOSS
BLAM
BLAM
CRASH

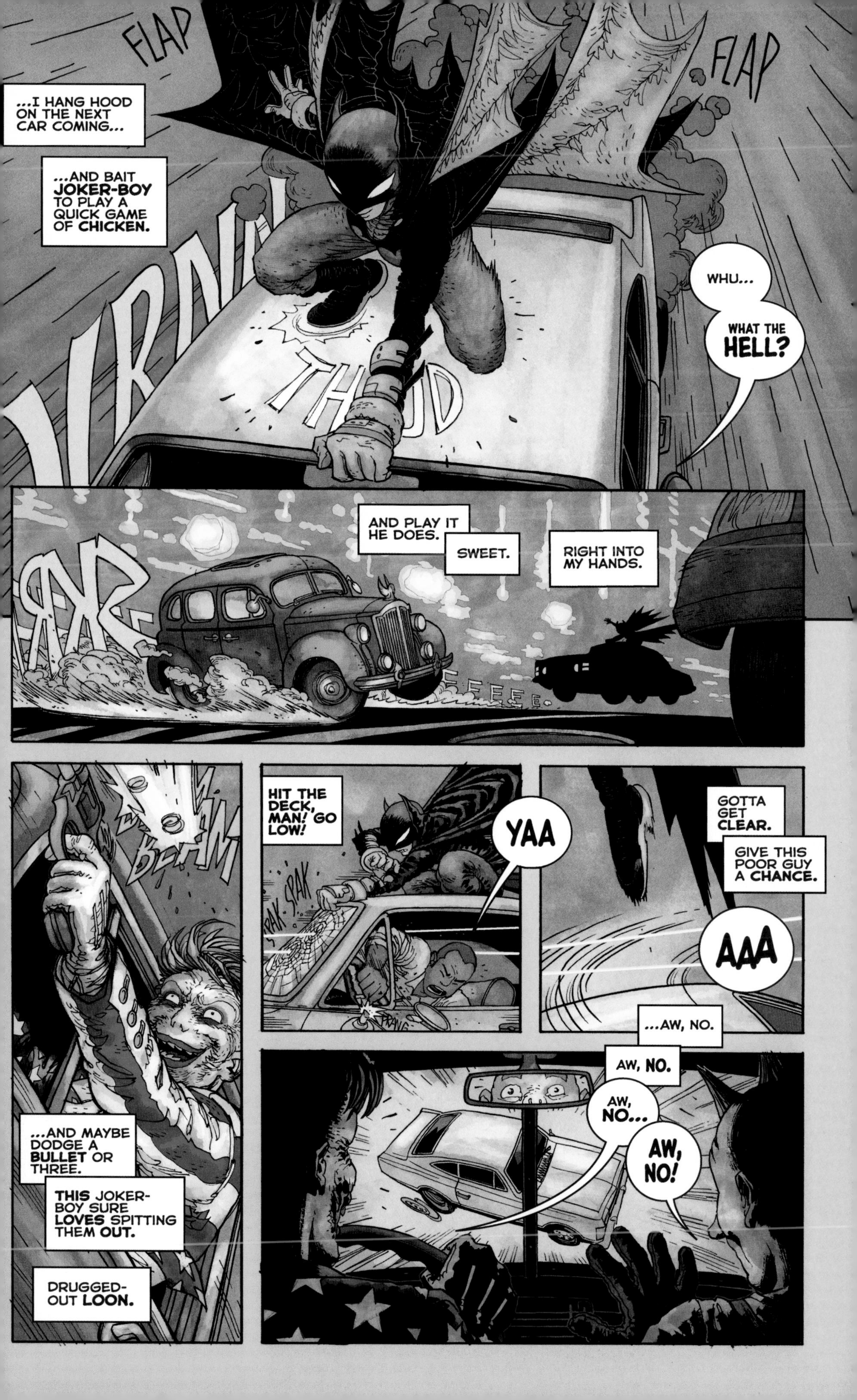
FLAP
FLAP
...I HANG HOOD ON THE NEXT CAR COMING...
...AND BAIT JOKER-BOY TO PLAY A QUICK GAME OF CHICKEN.
THUD
WHU...
WHAT THE HELL?
AND PLAY IT HE DOES.
SWEET.
RIGHT INTO MY HANDS.
...AND MAYBE DODGE A BULLET OR THREE.
THIS JOKER-BOY SURE LOVES SPITTING THEM OUT.
DRUGGED-OUT LOON.
HIT THE DECK, MAN! GO LOW!
YAA
SPAK SPAK
GOTTA GET CLEAR.
GIVE THIS POOR GUY A CHANCE.
AAA
...AW, NO.
AW, NO.
AW, NO...
AW, NO!

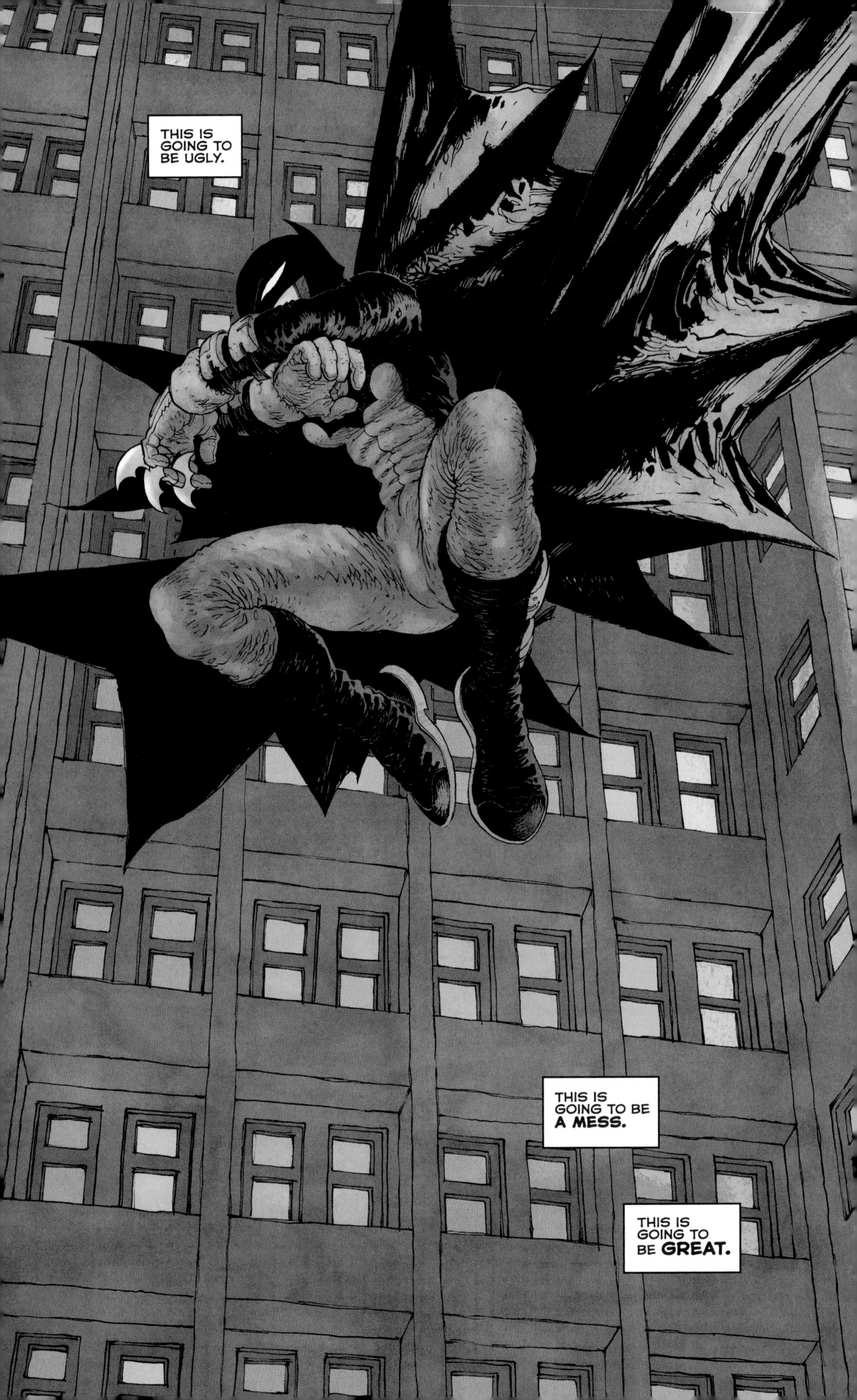
THIS IS GOING TO BE UGLY.
THIS IS GOING TO BE A MESS.
THIS IS GOING TO BE GREAT.

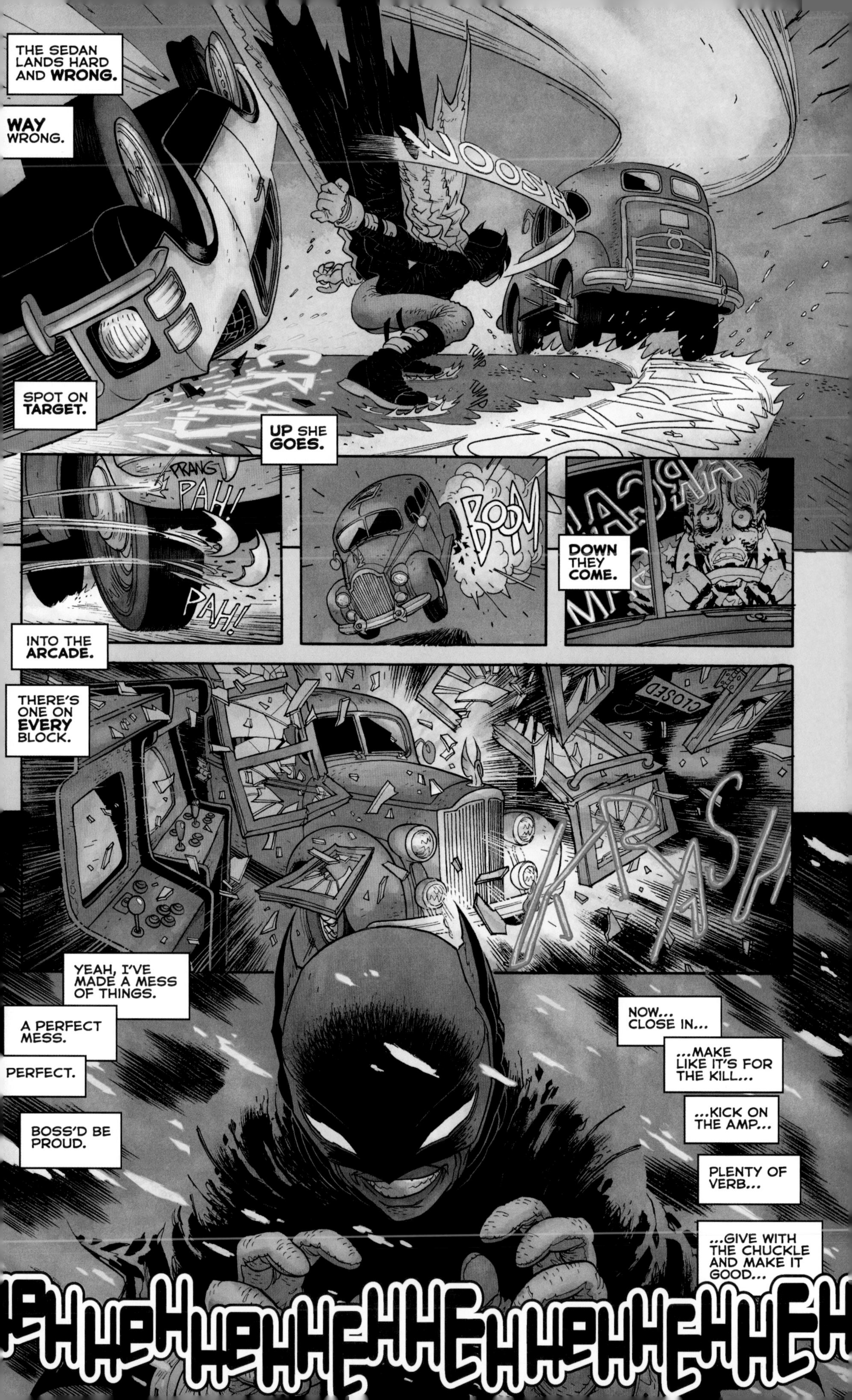
THE SEDAN LANDS HARD AND WRONG.
WAY WRONG.
WOOSH
SPOT ON TARGET.
TUMP
TUMP
UP SHE GOES.
PRANG
PAH!
PAH!
BOOM
DOWN THEY COME.
INTO THE ARCADE.
THERE'S ONE ON EVERY BLOCK.
CLOSED
KRASH
YEAH, I'VE MADE A MESS OF THINGS.
A PERFECT MESS.
PERFECT.
BOSS'D BE PROUD.
NOW... CLOSE IN...
...MAKE LIKE IT'S FOR THE KILL...
...KICK ON THE AMP...
PLENTY OF VERB...
...GIVE WITH THE CHUCKLE AND MAKE IT GOOD...

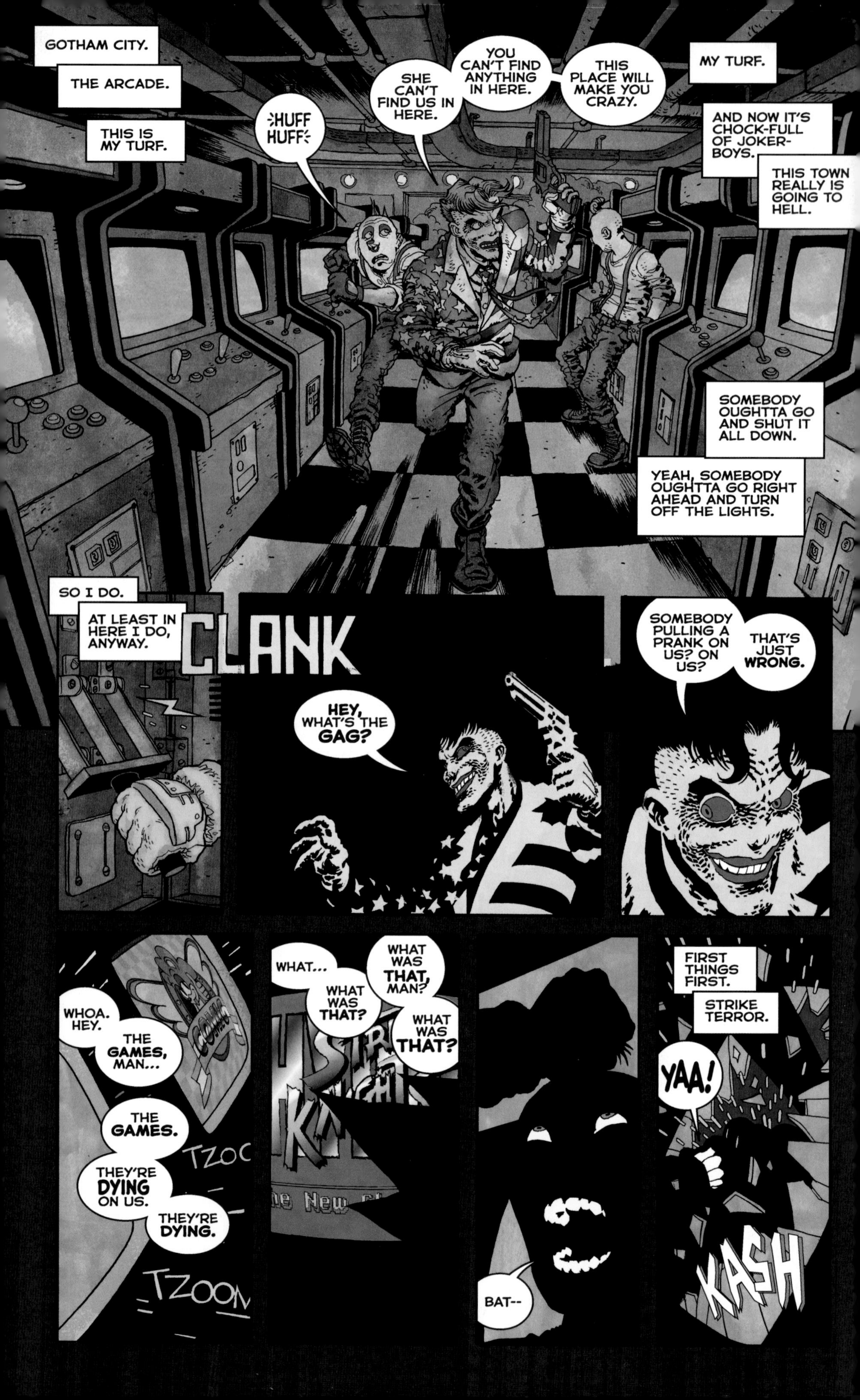
GOTHAM CITY.
THE ARCADE.
THIS IS MY TURF.
HUFF HUFF
SHE CAN'T FIND US IN HERE.
YOU CAN'T FIND ANYTHING IN HERE.
THIS PLACE WILL MAKE YOU CRAZY.
MY TURF.
AND NOW IT'S CHOCK-FULL OF JOKER-BOYS.
THIS TOWN REALLY IS GOING TO HELL.
SOMEBODY OUGHTTA GO AND SHUT IT ALL DOWN.
YEAH, SOMEBODY OUGHTTA GO RIGHT AHEAD AND TURN OFF THE LIGHTS.
SO I DO.
AT LEAST IN HERE I DO, ANYWAY.
CLANK
HEY, WHAT'S THE GAG?
SOMEBODY PULLING A PRANK ON US? ON US?
THAT'S JUST WRONG.
WHOA. HEY.
THE GAMES, MAN...
THE GAMES.
THEY'RE DYING ON US.
THEY'RE DYING.
TZOOM
WHAT...
WHAT WAS THAT?
WHAT WAS THAT, MAN?
WHAT WAS THAT?
BAT--
FIRST THINGS FIRST.
STRIKE TERROR.
YAA!
KASH

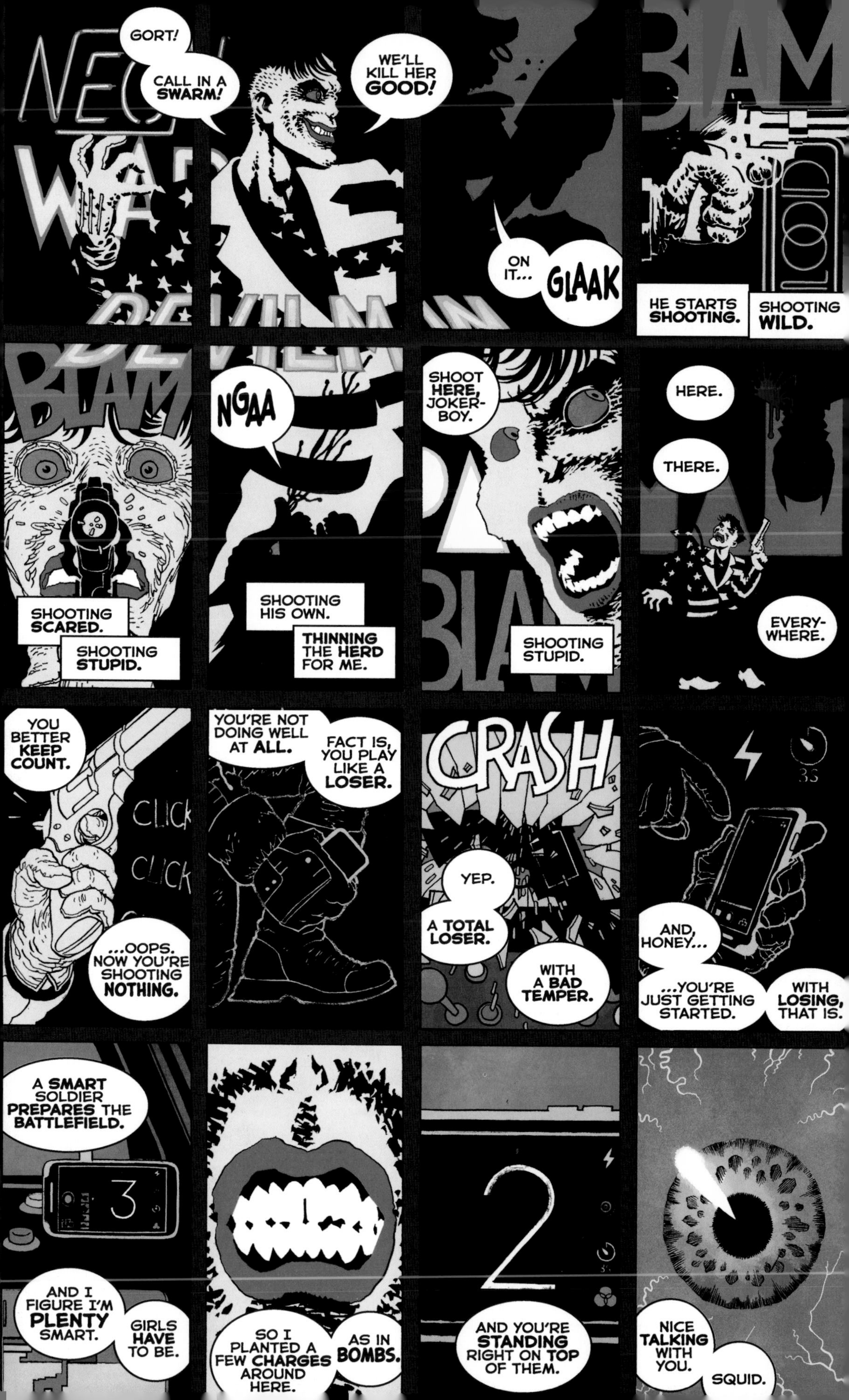
GORT!
CALL IN A SWARM!
WE'LL KILL HER GOOD!
ON IT...
GLAAK
BLAM
HE STARTS SHOOTING.
SHOOTING WILD.
BLAM
SHOOTING SCARED.
SHOOTING STUPID.
NGAA
SHOOTING HIS OWN.
THINNING THE HERD FOR ME.
SHOOT HERE, JOKER-BOY.
SHOOTING STUPID.
HERE.
THERE.
EVERY-WHERE.
YOU BETTER KEEP COUNT.
CLICK
CLICK
...OOPS. NOW YOU'RE SHOOTING NOTHING.
YOU'RE NOT DOING WELL AT ALL.
FACT IS, YOU PLAY LIKE A LOSER.
CRASH
YEP.
A TOTAL LOSER.
WITH A BAD TEMPER.
AND, HONEY...
...YOU'RE JUST GETTING STARTED.
WITH LOSING, THAT IS.
A SMART SOLDIER PREPARES THE BATTLEFIELD.
3
AND I FIGURE I'M PLENTY SMART.
GIRLS HAVE TO BE.
SO I PLANTED A FEW CHARGES AROUND HERE.
AS IN BOMBS.
2
AND YOU'RE STANDING RIGHT ON TOP OF THEM.
NICE TALKING WITH YOU.
SQUID.

I RIDE A FIREBALL.

THE BATWOMAN

FLASH

MY KICK ALMOST TEARS HIS HEAD CLEAN OFF.

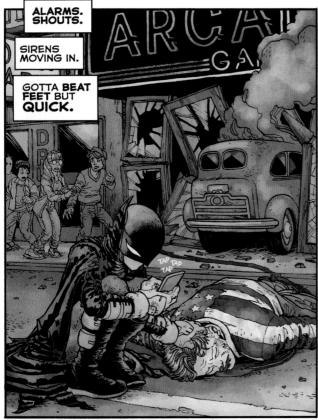

ALARMS. SHOUTS.

SIRENS MOVING IN.

GOTTA BEAT FEET BUT QUICK.

TAP TAP TAP

WOOP

TAP TAP

clow

WOO

clown down Boss

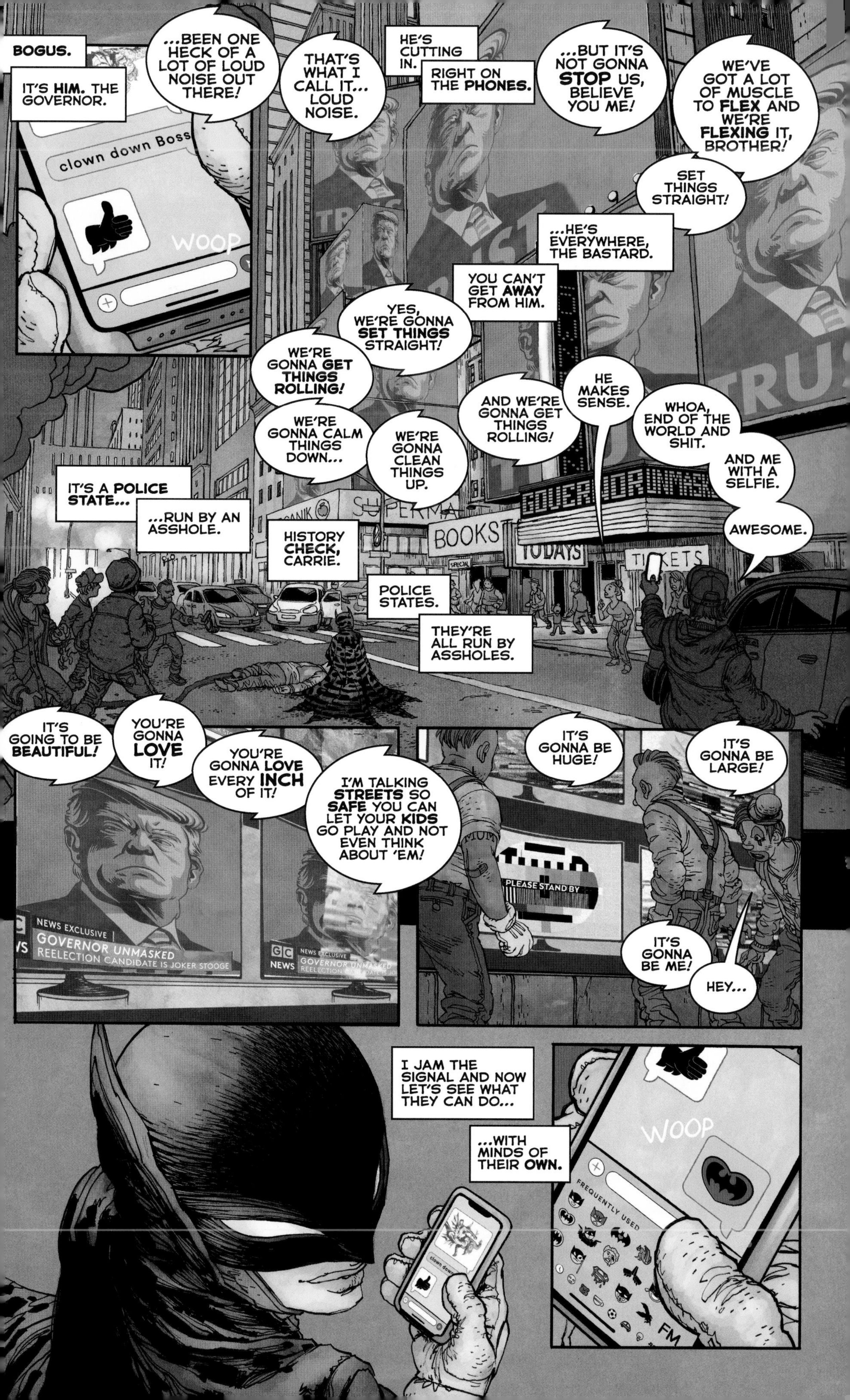
BOGUS.
IT'S HIM. THE GOVERNOR.
clown down Boss
WOOP
...BEEN ONE HECK OF A LOT OF LOUD NOISE OUT THERE!
THAT'S WHAT I CALL IT... LOUD NOISE.
HE'S CUTTING IN.
RIGHT ON THE PHONES.
...BUT IT'S NOT GONNA STOP US, BELIEVE YOU ME!
WE'VE GOT A LOT OF MUSCLE TO FLEX AND WE'RE FLEXING IT, BROTHER!
SET THINGS STRAIGHT!
...HE'S EVERYWHERE, THE BASTARD.
YOU CAN'T GET AWAY FROM HIM.
YES, WE'RE GONNA SET THINGS STRAIGHT!
WE'RE GONNA GET THINGS ROLLING!
WE'RE GONNA CALM THINGS DOWN...
WE'RE GONNA CLEAN THINGS UP.
AND WE'RE GONNA GET THINGS ROLLING!
HE MAKES SENSE.
WHOA, END OF THE WORLD AND SHIT.
AND ME WITH A SELFIE.
AWESOME.
IT'S A POLICE STATE...
...RUN BY AN ASSHOLE.
HISTORY CHECK, CARRIE.
POLICE STATES.
THEY'RE ALL RUN BY ASSHOLES.
BOOKS
TODAYS
TICKETS
IT'S GOING TO BE BEAUTIFUL!
YOU'RE GONNA LOVE IT!
YOU'RE GONNA LOVE EVERY INCH OF IT!
I'M TALKING STREETS SO SAFE YOU CAN LET YOUR KIDS GO PLAY AND NOT EVEN THINK ABOUT 'EM!
NEWS EXCLUSIVE
GOVERNOR UNMASKED
REELECTION CANDIDATE IS JOKER STOOGE
IT'S GONNA BE HUGE!
IT'S GONNA BE LARGE!
PLEASE STAND BY
IT'S GONNA BE ME!
HEY...
I JAM THE SIGNAL AND NOW LET'S SEE WHAT THEY CAN DO...
...WITH MINDS OF THEIR OWN.
WOOP
FREQUENTLY USED

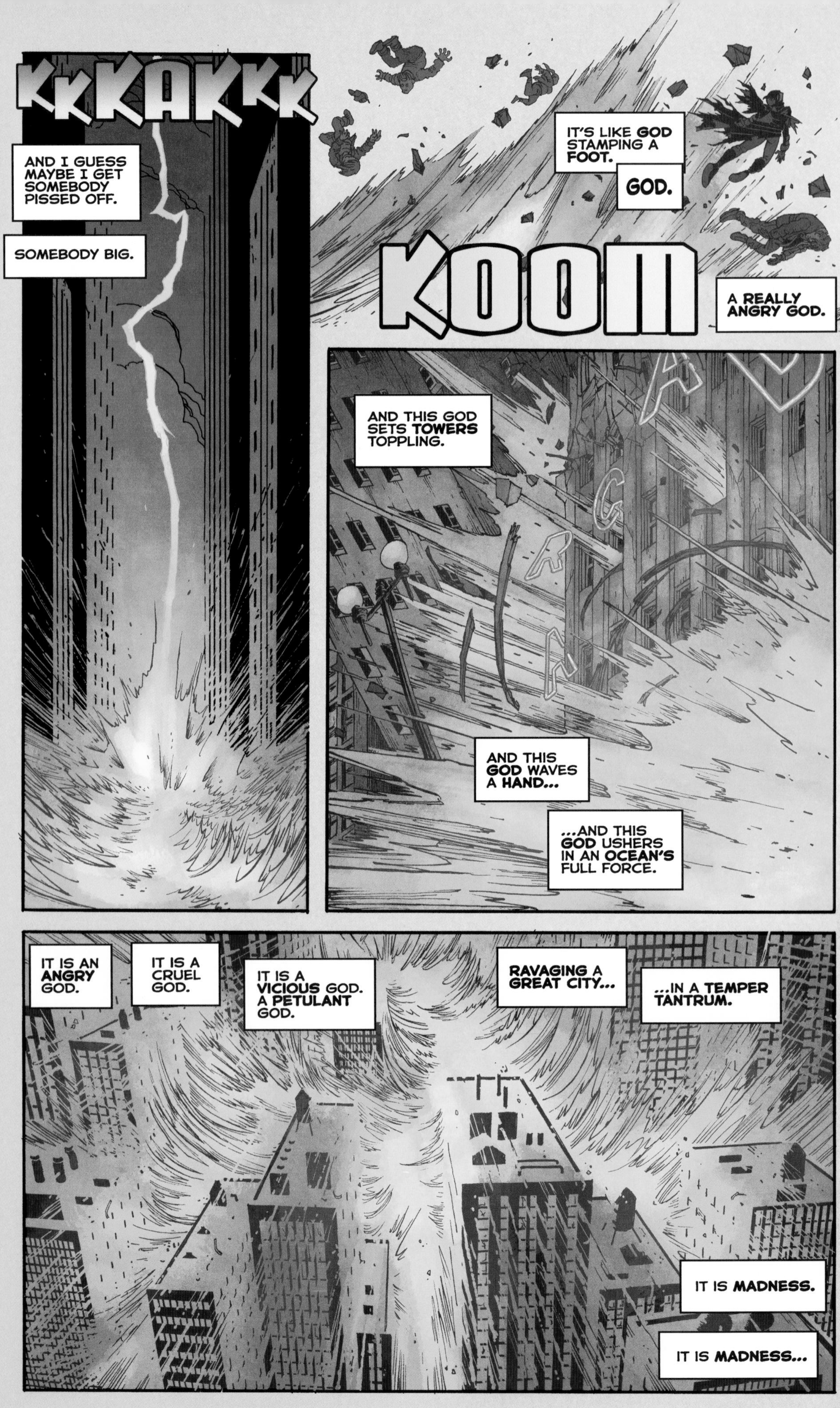
KKKAKKK
AND I GUESS MAYBE I GET SOMEBODY PISSED OFF.
SOMEBODY BIG.
IT'S LIKE GOD STAMPING A FOOT.
GOD.
KOOM
A REALLY ANGRY GOD.
AND THIS GOD SETS TOWERS TOPPLING.
AND THIS GOD WAVES A HAND...
...AND THIS GOD USHERS IN AN OCEAN'S FULL FORCE.
IT IS AN ANGRY GOD.
IT IS A CRUEL GOD.
IT IS A VICIOUS GOD. A PETULANT GOD.
RAVAGING A GREAT CITY...
...IN A TEMPER TANTRUM.
IT IS MADNESS.
IT IS MADNESS...

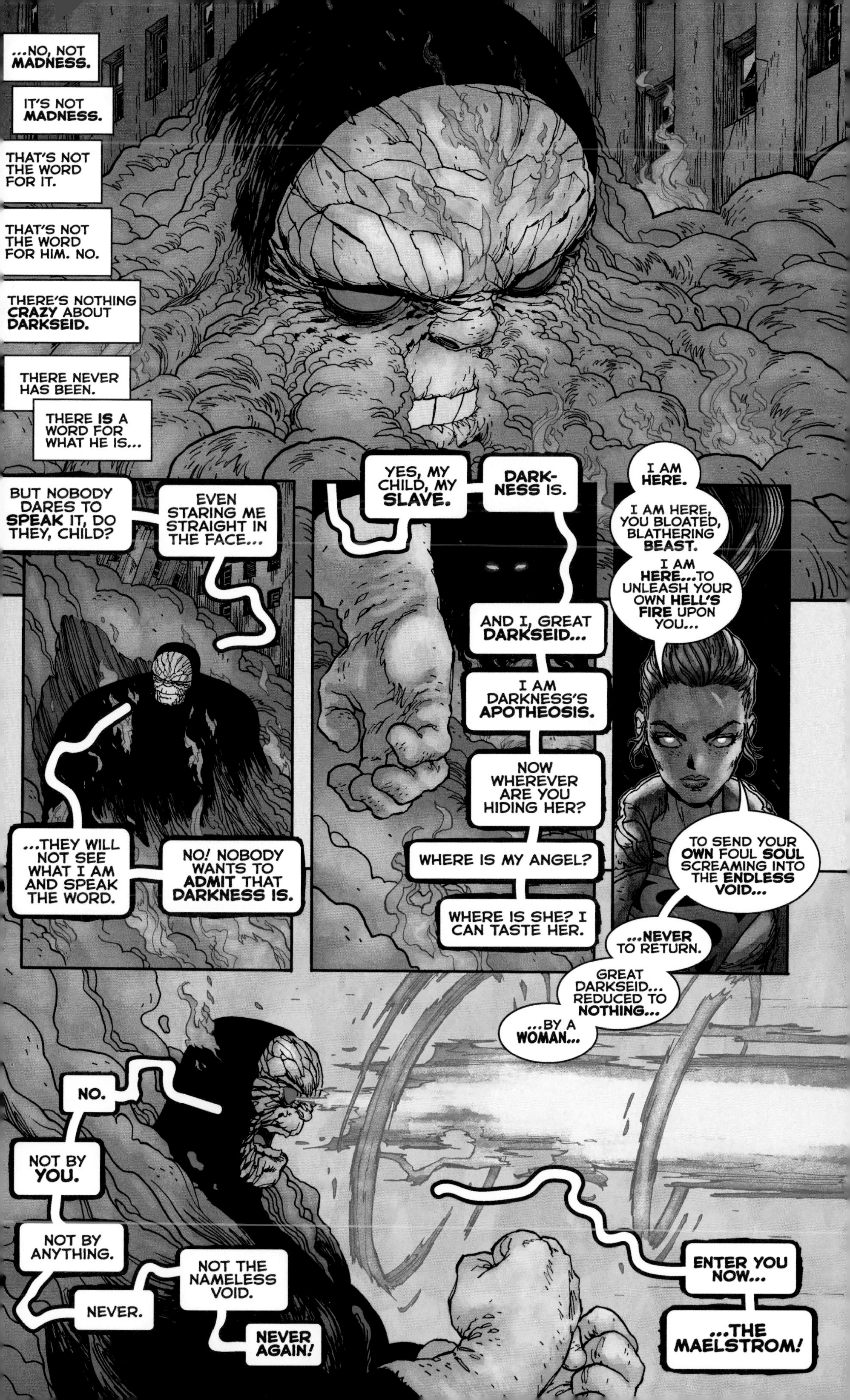
...NO, NOT MADNESS.
IT'S NOT MADNESS.
THAT'S NOT THE WORD FOR IT.
THAT'S NOT THE WORD FOR HIM. NO.
THERE'S NOTHING CRAZY ABOUT DARKSEID.
THERE NEVER HAS BEEN.
THERE IS A WORD FOR WHAT HE IS...
BUT NOBODY DARES TO SPEAK IT, DO THEY, CHILD?
EVEN STARING ME STRAIGHT IN THE FACE...
...THEY WILL NOT SEE WHAT I AM AND SPEAK THE WORD.
NO! NOBODY WANTS TO ADMIT THAT DARKNESS IS.
YES, MY CHILD, MY SLAVE.
DARK-NESS IS.
AND I, GREAT DARKSEID...
I AM DARKNESS'S APOTHEOSIS.
NOW WHEREVER ARE YOU HIDING HER?
WHERE IS MY ANGEL?
WHERE IS SHE? I CAN TASTE HER.
I AM HERE.
I AM HERE, YOU BLOATED, BLATHERING BEAST.
I AM HERE...TO UNLEASH YOUR OWN HELL'S FIRE UPON YOU...
TO SEND YOUR OWN FOUL SOUL SCREAMING INTO THE ENDLESS VOID...
...NEVER TO RETURN.
GREAT DARKSEID... REDUCED TO NOTHING...
...BY A WOMAN...
NO.
NOT BY YOU.
NOT BY ANYTHING.
NEVER.
NOT THE NAMELESS VOID.
NEVER AGAIN!
ENTER YOU NOW...
...THE MAELSTROM!

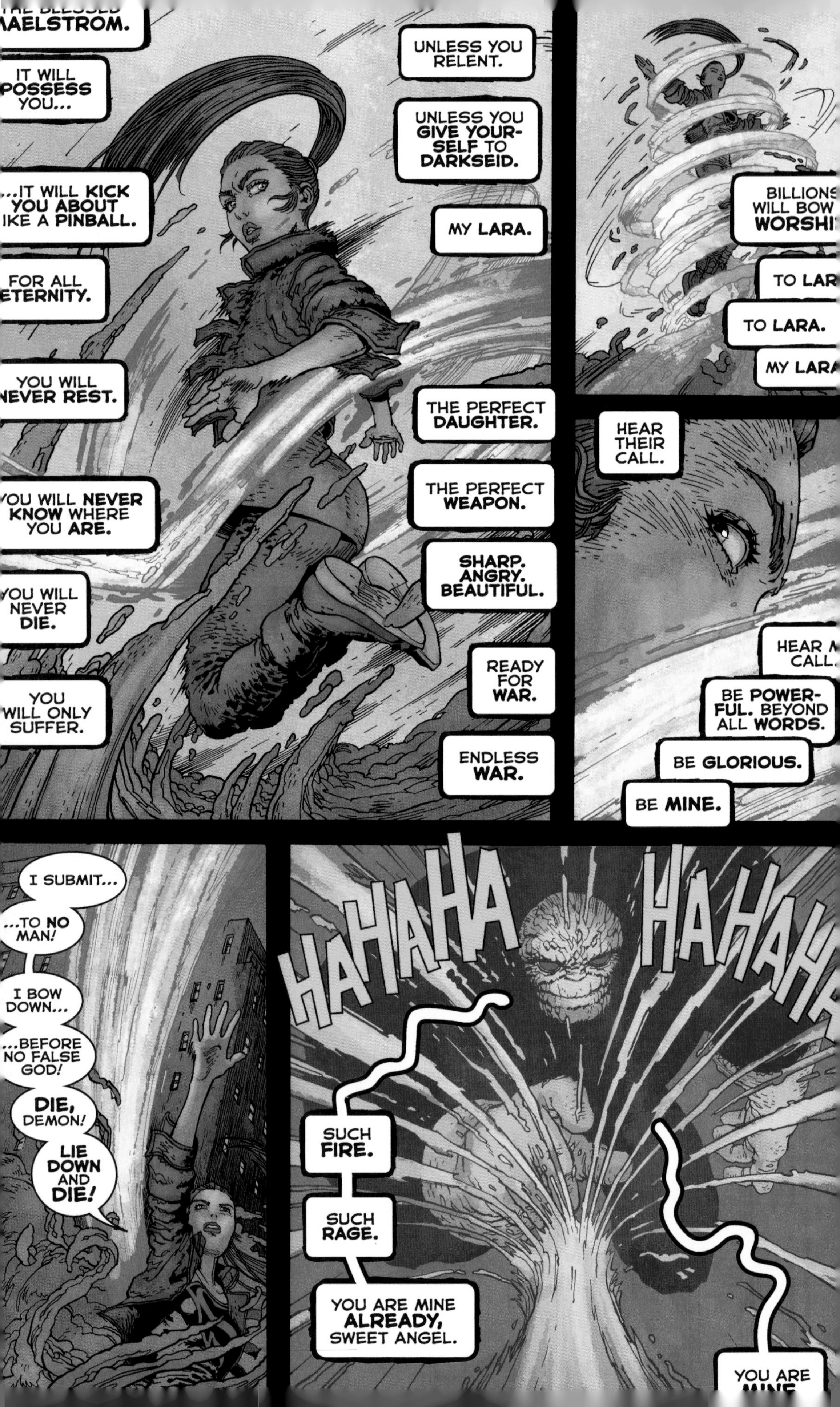

AELSTROM.
IT WILL POSSESS YOU...
...IT WILL KICK YOU ABOUT IKE A PINBALL.
FOR ALL ETERNITY.
YOU WILL NEVER REST.
YOU WILL NEVER KNOW WHERE YOU ARE.
YOU WILL NEVER DIE.
YOU WILL ONLY SUFFER.
UNLESS YOU RELENT.
UNLESS YOU GIVE YOURSELF TO DARKSEID.
MY LARA.
THE PERFECT DAUGHTER.
THE PERFECT WEAPON.
SHARP. ANGRY. BEAUTIFUL.
READY FOR WAR.
ENDLESS WAR.
BILLIONS WILL BOW WORSHI
TO LAR
TO LARA.
MY LARA
HEAR THEIR CALL.
HEAR M CALL.
BE POWERFUL. BEYOND ALL WORDS.
BE GLORIOUS.
BE MINE.
I SUBMIT...
...TO NO MAN!
I BOW DOWN...
...BEFORE NO FALSE GOD!
DIE, DEMON!
LIE DOWN AND DIE!
HAHAHA
HAHAHA
SUCH FIRE.
SUCH RAGE.
YOU ARE MINE ALREADY, SWEET ANGEL.
YOU ARE

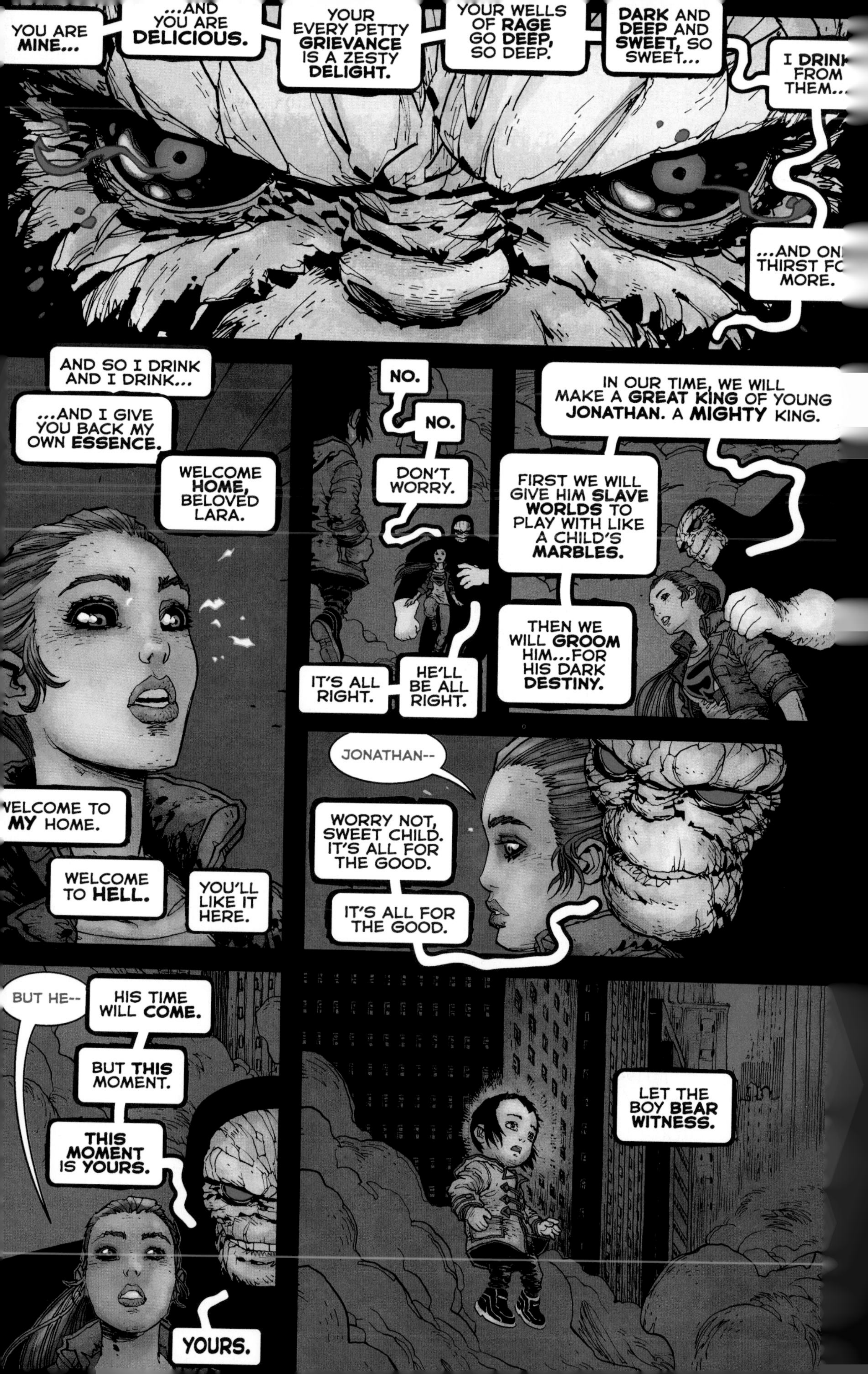

YOU ARE MINE...
...AND YOU ARE DELICIOUS.
YOUR EVERY PETTY GRIEVANCE IS A ZESTY DELIGHT.
YOUR WELLS OF RAGE GO DEEP, SO DEEP.
DARK AND DEEP AND SWEET, SO SWEET...
I DRINK FROM THEM...
...AND ONLY THIRST FOR MORE.
AND SO I DRINK AND I DRINK...
...AND I GIVE YOU BACK MY OWN ESSENCE.
WELCOME HOME, BELOVED LARA.
WELCOME TO MY HOME.
WELCOME TO HELL.
YOU'LL LIKE IT HERE.
NO.
NO.
DON'T WORRY.
IT'S ALL RIGHT.
HE'LL BE ALL RIGHT.
IN OUR TIME, WE WILL MAKE A GREAT KING OF YOUNG JONATHAN. A MIGHTY KING.
FIRST WE WILL GIVE HIM SLAVE WORLDS TO PLAY WITH LIKE A CHILD'S MARBLES.
THEN WE WILL GROOM HIM...FOR HIS DARK DESTINY.
JONATHAN--
WORRY NOT, SWEET CHILD. IT'S ALL FOR THE GOOD.
IT'S ALL FOR THE GOOD.
BUT HE--
HIS TIME WILL COME.
BUT THIS MOMENT.
THIS MOMENT IS YOURS.
YOURS.
LET THE BOY BEAR WITNESS.

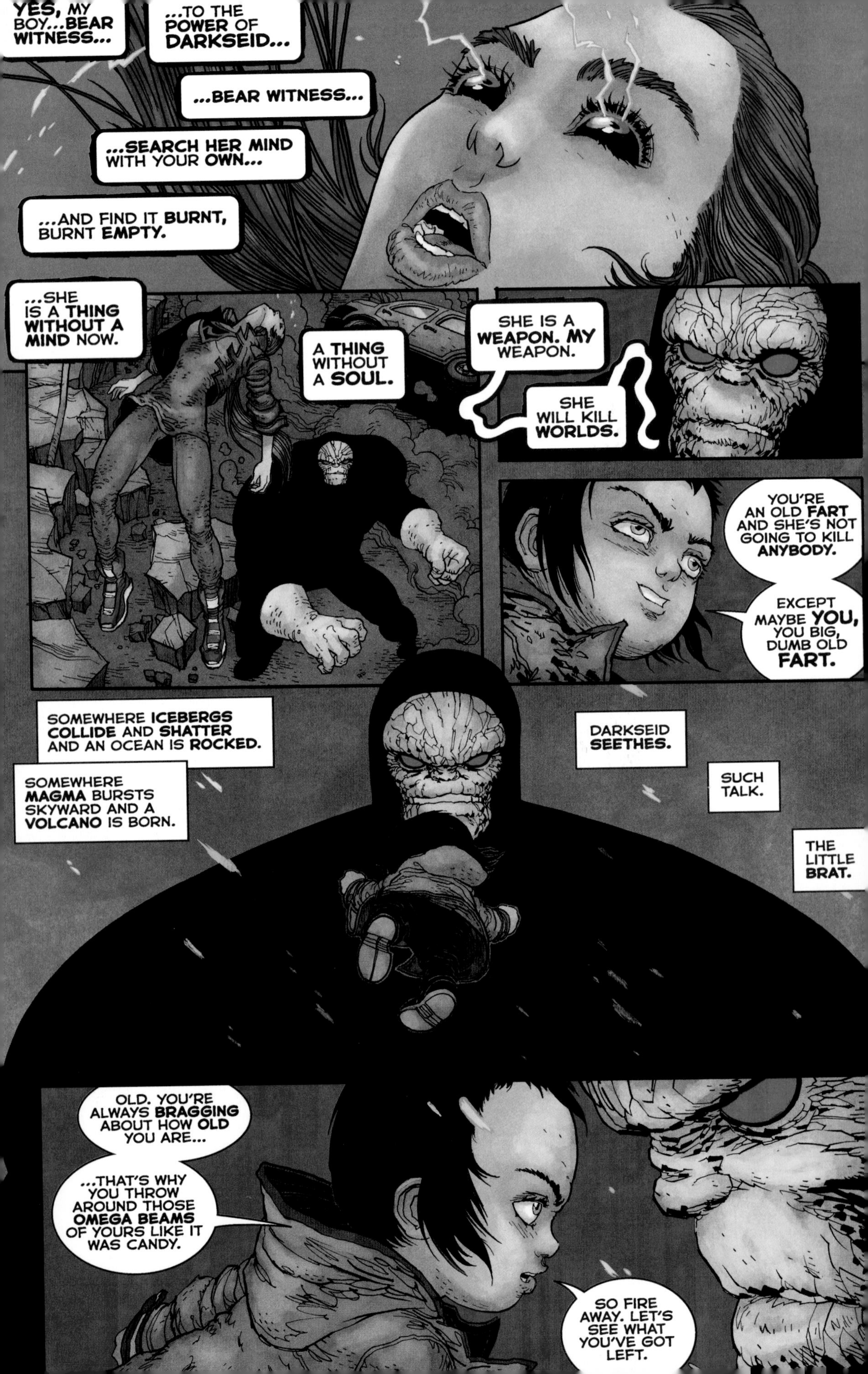
YES, MY BOY...BEAR WITNESS...
...TO THE POWER OF DARKSEID...
...BEAR WITNESS...
...SEARCH HER MIND WITH YOUR OWN...
...AND FIND IT BURNT, BURNT EMPTY.
...SHE IS A THING WITHOUT A MIND NOW.
A THING WITHOUT A SOUL.
SHE IS A WEAPON. MY WEAPON.
SHE WILL KILL WORLDS.
YOU'RE AN OLD FART AND SHE'S NOT GOING TO KILL ANYBODY.
EXCEPT MAYBE YOU, YOU BIG, DUMB OLD FART.
SOMEWHERE ICEBERGS COLLIDE AND SHATTER AND AN OCEAN IS ROCKED.
SOMEWHERE MAGMA BURSTS SKYWARD AND A VOLCANO IS BORN.
DARKSEID SEETHES.
SUCH TALK.
THE LITTLE BRAT.
OLD. YOU'RE ALWAYS BRAGGING ABOUT HOW OLD YOU ARE...
...THAT'S WHY YOU THROW AROUND THOSE OMEGA BEAMS OF YOURS LIKE IT WAS CANDY.
SO FIRE AWAY. LET'S SEE WHAT YOU'VE GOT LEFT.

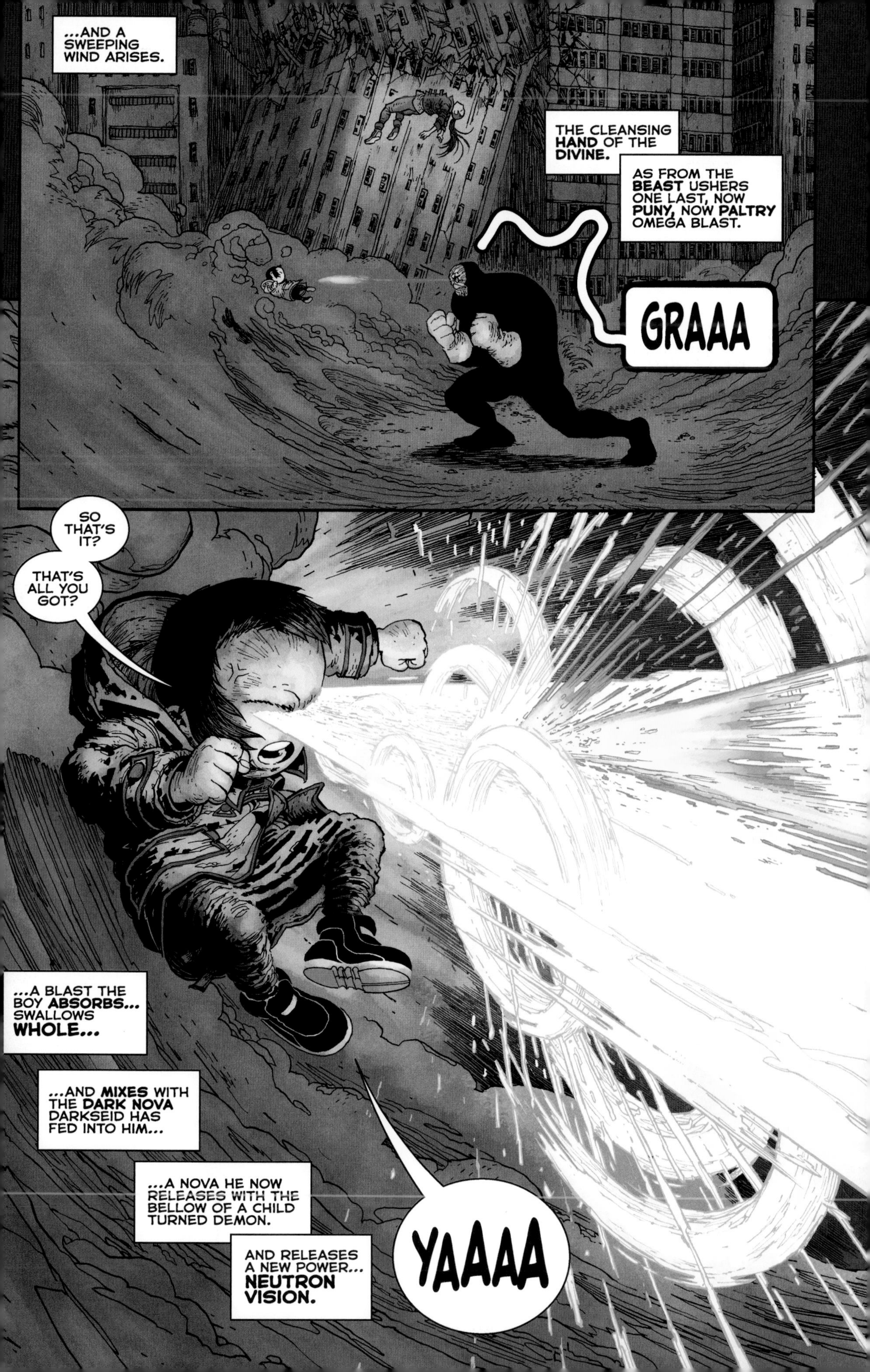
...AND A SWEEPING WIND ARISES.
THE CLEANSING HAND OF THE DIVINE.
AS FROM THE BEAST USHERS ONE LAST, NOW PUNY, NOW PALTRY OMEGA BLAST.
GRAAA
SO THAT'S IT?
THAT'S ALL YOU GOT?
...A BLAST THE BOY ABSORBS... SWALLOWS WHOLE...
...AND MIXES WITH THE DARK NOVA DARKSEID HAS FED INTO HIM...
...A NOVA HE NOW RELEASES WITH THE BELLOW OF A CHILD TURNED DEMON.
AND RELEASES A NEW POWER... NEUTRON VISION.
YAAAA

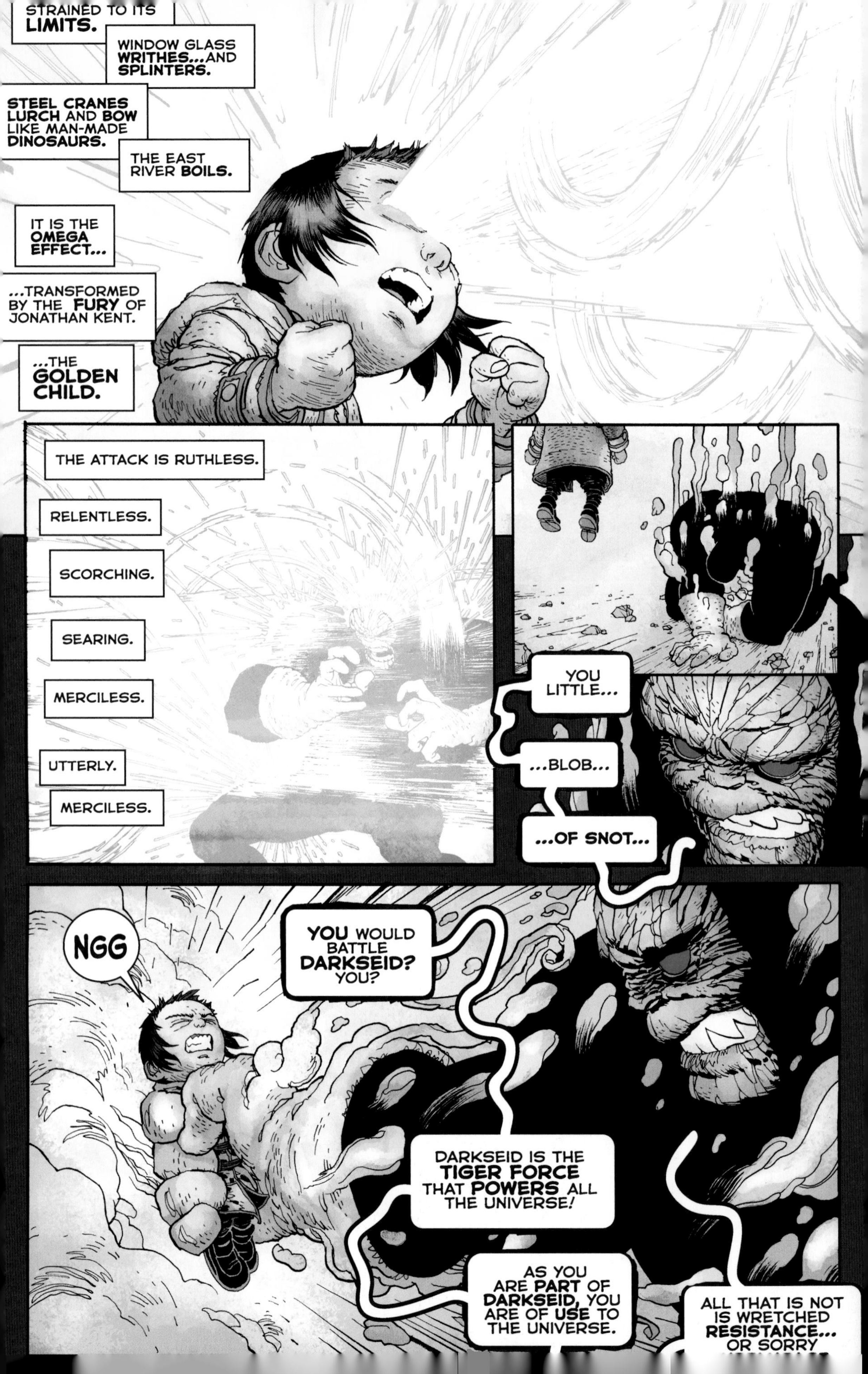
STRAINED TO ITS LIMITS.
WINDOW GLASS WRITHES...AND SPLINTERS.
STEEL CRANES LURCH AND BOW LIKE MAN-MADE DINOSAURS.
THE EAST RIVER BOILS.
IT IS THE OMEGA EFFECT...
...TRANSFORMED BY THE FURY OF JONATHAN KENT.
...THE GOLDEN CHILD.
THE ATTACK IS RUTHLESS.
RELENTLESS.
SCORCHING.
SEARING.
MERCILESS.
UTTERLY.
MERCILESS.
YOU LITTLE...
...BLOB...
...OF SNOT...
NGG
YOU WOULD BATTLE DARKSEID? YOU?
DARKSEID IS THE TIGER FORCE THAT POWERS ALL THE UNIVERSE!
AS YOU ARE PART OF DARKSEID, YOU ARE OF USE TO THE UNIVERSE.
ALL THAT IS NOT IS WRETCHED RESISTANCE... OR SORRY

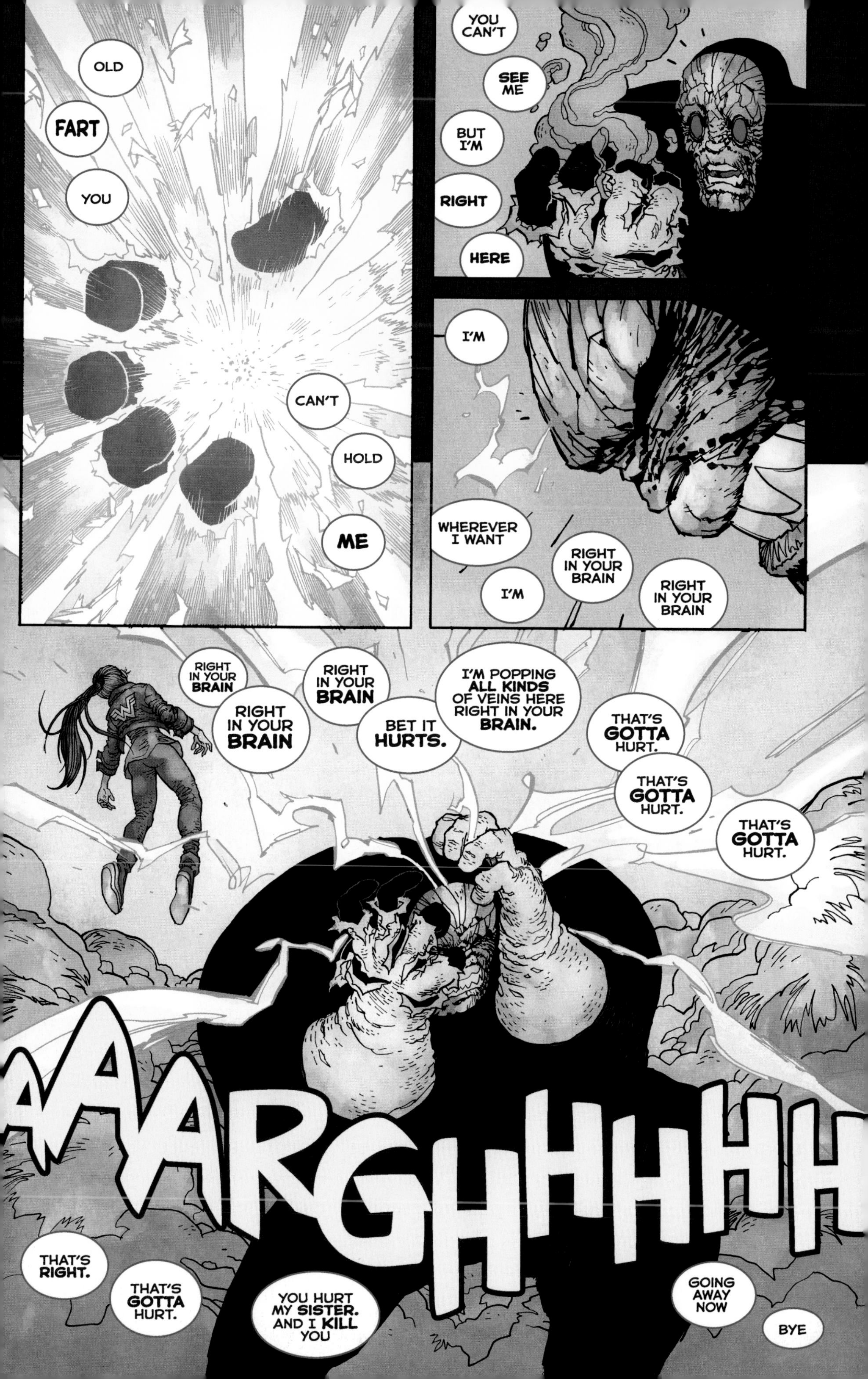
OLD
FART
YOU
CAN'T
HOLD
ME
YOU CAN'T
SEE ME
BUT I'M
RIGHT
HERE
I'M
WHEREVER I WANT
I'M
RIGHT IN YOUR BRAIN
RIGHT IN YOUR BRAIN
RIGHT IN YOUR BRAIN
RIGHT IN YOUR BRAIN
RIGHT IN YOUR BRAIN
BET IT HURTS.
I'M POPPING ALL KINDS OF VEINS HERE RIGHT IN YOUR BRAIN.
THAT'S GOTTA HURT.
THAT'S GOTTA HURT.
THAT'S GOTTA HURT.
AAARGHHHHH
THAT'S RIGHT.
THAT'S GOTTA HURT.
YOU HURT MY SISTER. AND I KILL YOU
GOING AWAY NOW
BYE

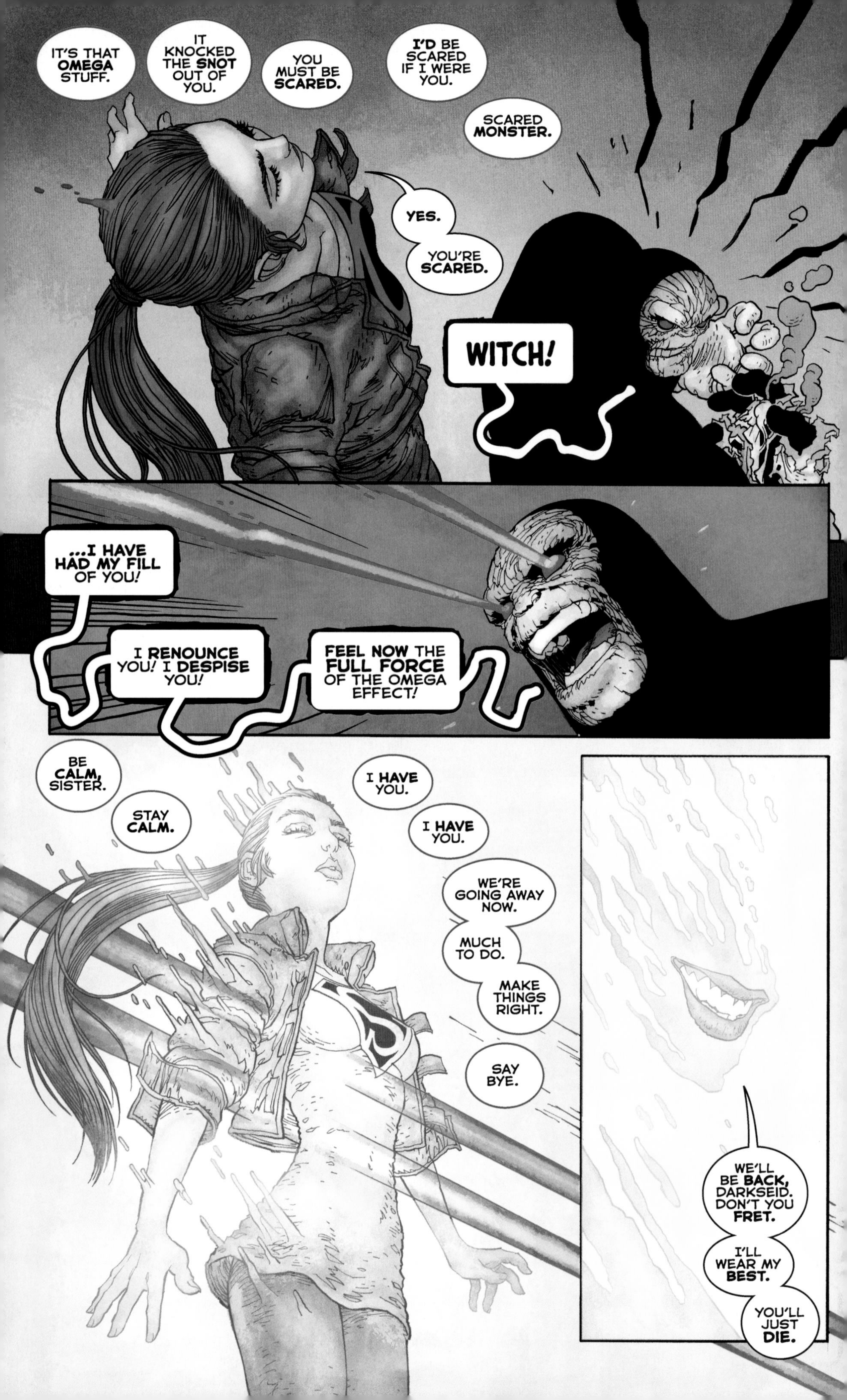
IT'S THAT OMEGA STUFF.
IT KNOCKED THE SNOT OUT OF YOU.
YOU MUST BE SCARED.
I'D BE SCARED IF I WERE YOU.
SCARED MONSTER.
YES.
YOU'RE SCARED.
WITCH!
...I HAVE HAD MY FILL OF YOU!
I RENOUNCE YOU! I DESPISE YOU!
FEEL NOW THE FULL FORCE OF THE OMEGA EFFECT!
BE CALM, SISTER.
STAY CALM.
I HAVE YOU.
I HAVE YOU.
WE'RE GOING AWAY NOW.
MUCH TO DO.
MAKE THINGS RIGHT.
SAY BYE.
WE'LL BE BACK, DARKSEID. DON'T YOU FRET.
I'LL WEAR MY BEST.
YOU'LL JUST DIE.

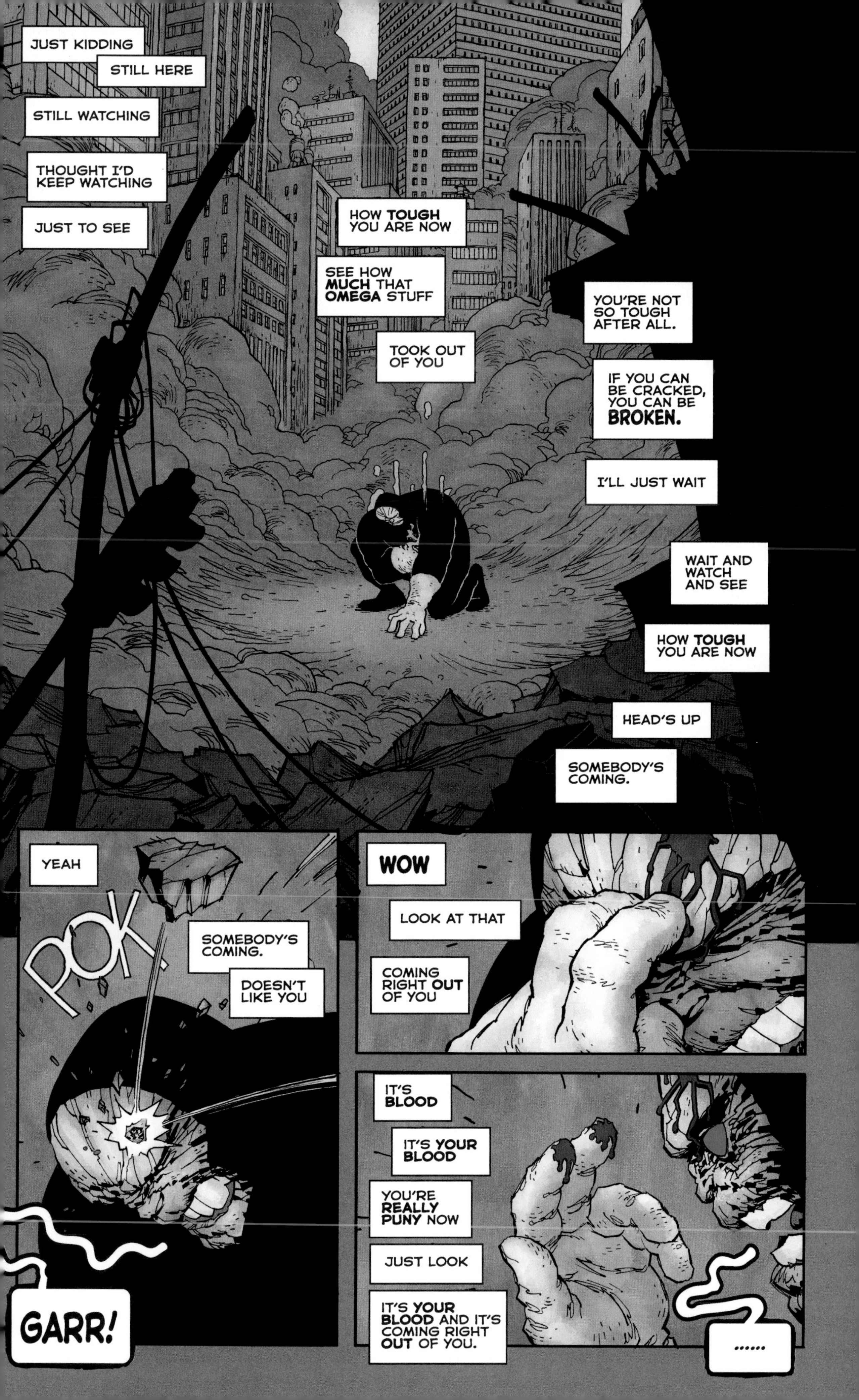
JUST KIDDING
STILL HERE
STILL WATCHING
THOUGHT I'D KEEP WATCHING
JUST TO SEE
HOW **TOUGH** YOU ARE NOW
SEE HOW **MUCH** THAT **OMEGA** STUFF
TOOK OUT OF YOU
YOU'RE NOT SO TOUGH AFTER ALL.
IF YOU CAN BE CRACKED, YOU CAN BE **BROKEN.**
I'LL JUST WAIT
WAIT AND WATCH AND SEE
HOW **TOUGH** YOU ARE NOW
HEAD'S UP
SOMEBODY'S COMING.
YEAH
POK
SOMEBODY'S COMING.
DOESN'T LIKE YOU
GARR!
WOW
LOOK AT THAT
COMING RIGHT **OUT** OF YOU
IT'S **BLOOD**
IT'S **YOUR BLOOD**
YOU'RE **REALLY PUNY** NOW
JUST LOOK
IT'S **YOUR BLOOD** AND IT'S COMING RIGHT **OUT** OF YOU.
......

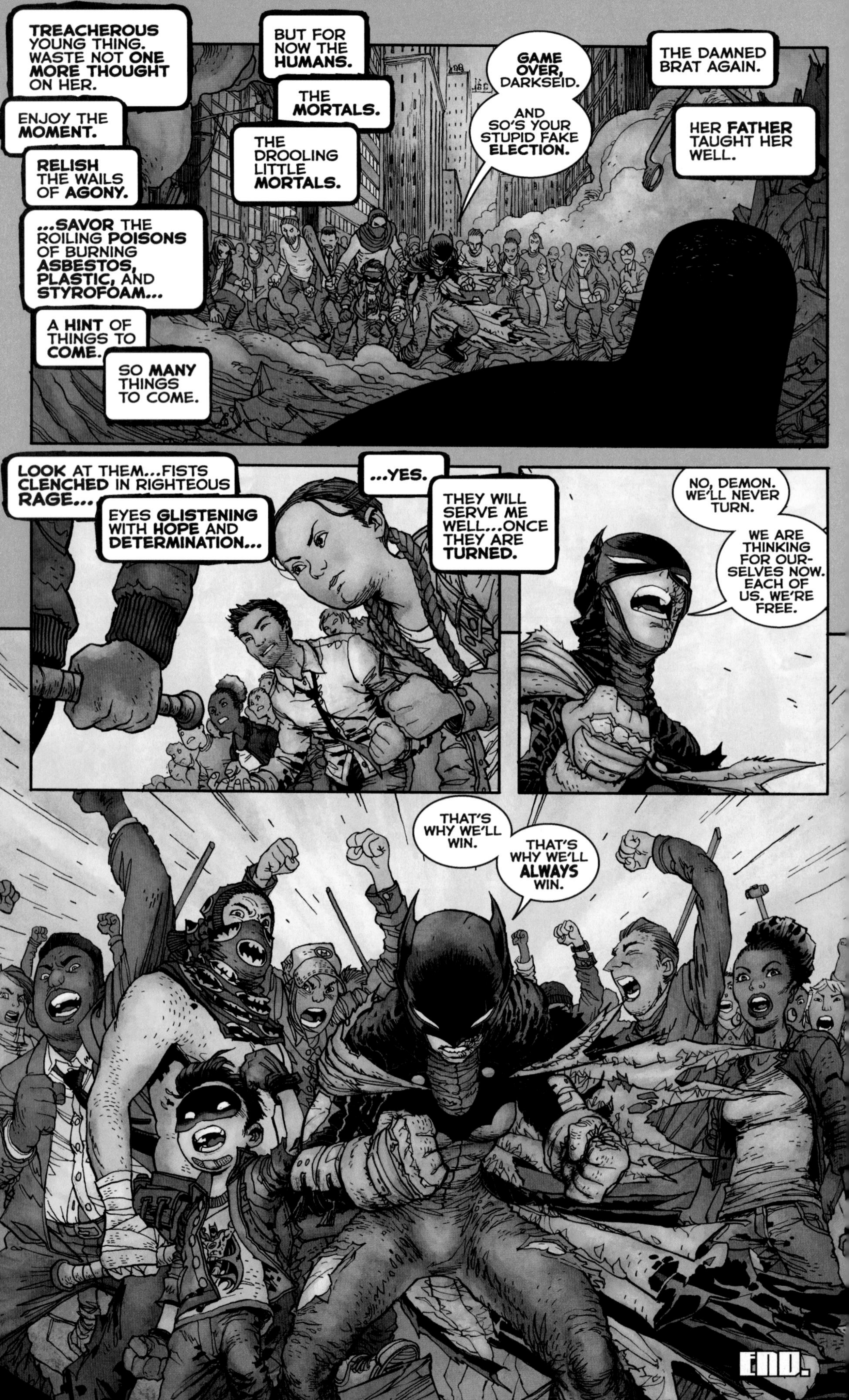
TREACHEROUS YOUNG THING. WASTE NOT ONE MORE THOUGHT ON HER.
ENJOY THE MOMENT.
RELISH THE WAILS OF AGONY.
...SAVOR THE ROILING POISONS OF BURNING ASBESTOS, PLASTIC, AND STYROFOAM...
A HINT OF THINGS TO COME.
SO MANY THINGS TO COME.
BUT FOR NOW THE HUMANS.
THE MORTALS.
THE DROOLING LITTLE MORTALS.
GAME OVER, DARKSEID.
AND SO'S YOUR STUPID FAKE ELECTION.
THE DAMNED BRAT AGAIN.
HER FATHER TAUGHT HER WELL.
LOOK AT THEM...FISTS CLENCHED IN RIGHTEOUS RAGE...
EYES GLISTENING WITH HOPE AND DETERMINATION...
...YES.
THEY WILL SERVE ME WELL...ONCE THEY ARE TURNED.
NO, DEMON. WE'LL NEVER TURN.
WE ARE THINKING FOR OUR-SELVES NOW. EACH OF US. WE'RE FREE.
THAT'S WHY WE'LL WIN.
THAT'S WHY WE'LL ALWAYS WIN.
END.

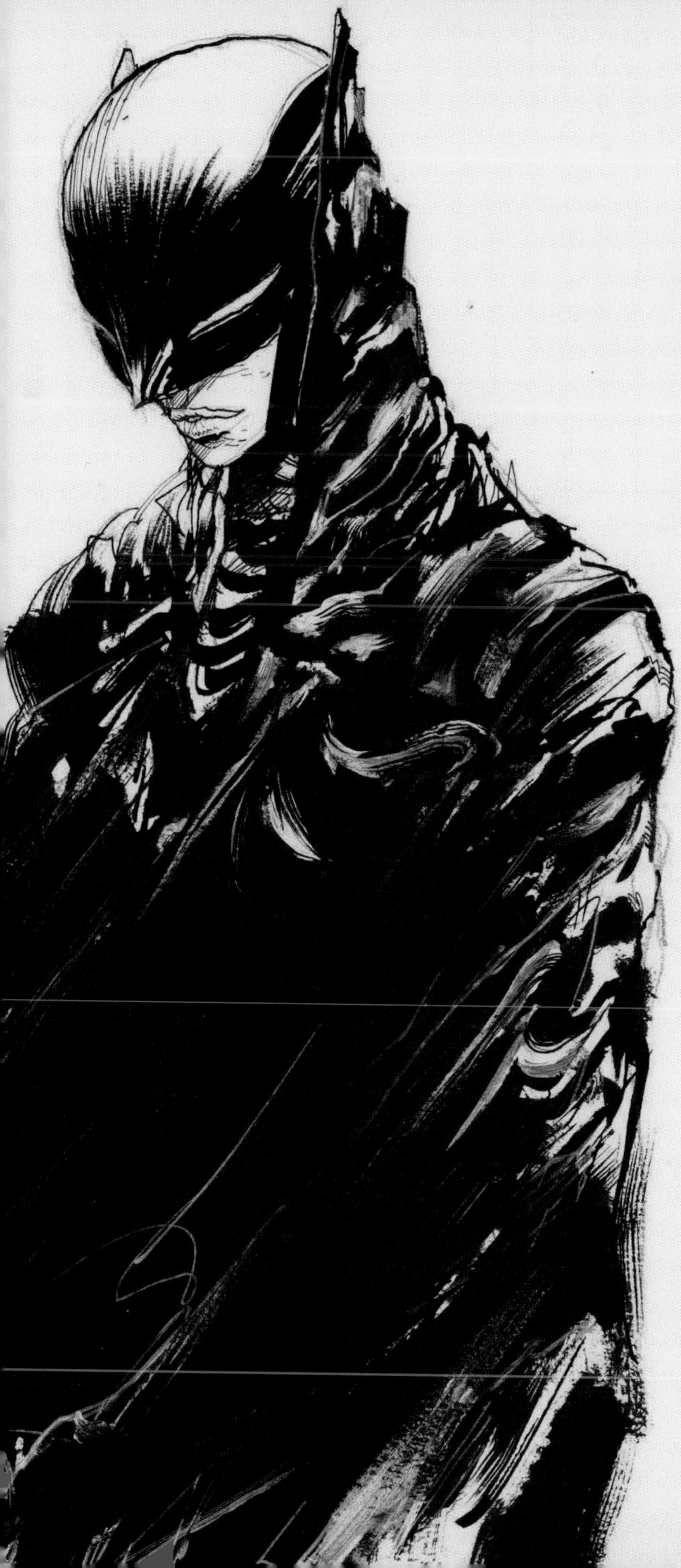

BONUS SECTION

Dark Knight Returns: The Golden Child №1 variant cover by RAFAEL GRAMPÁ with PEDRO COBIACO

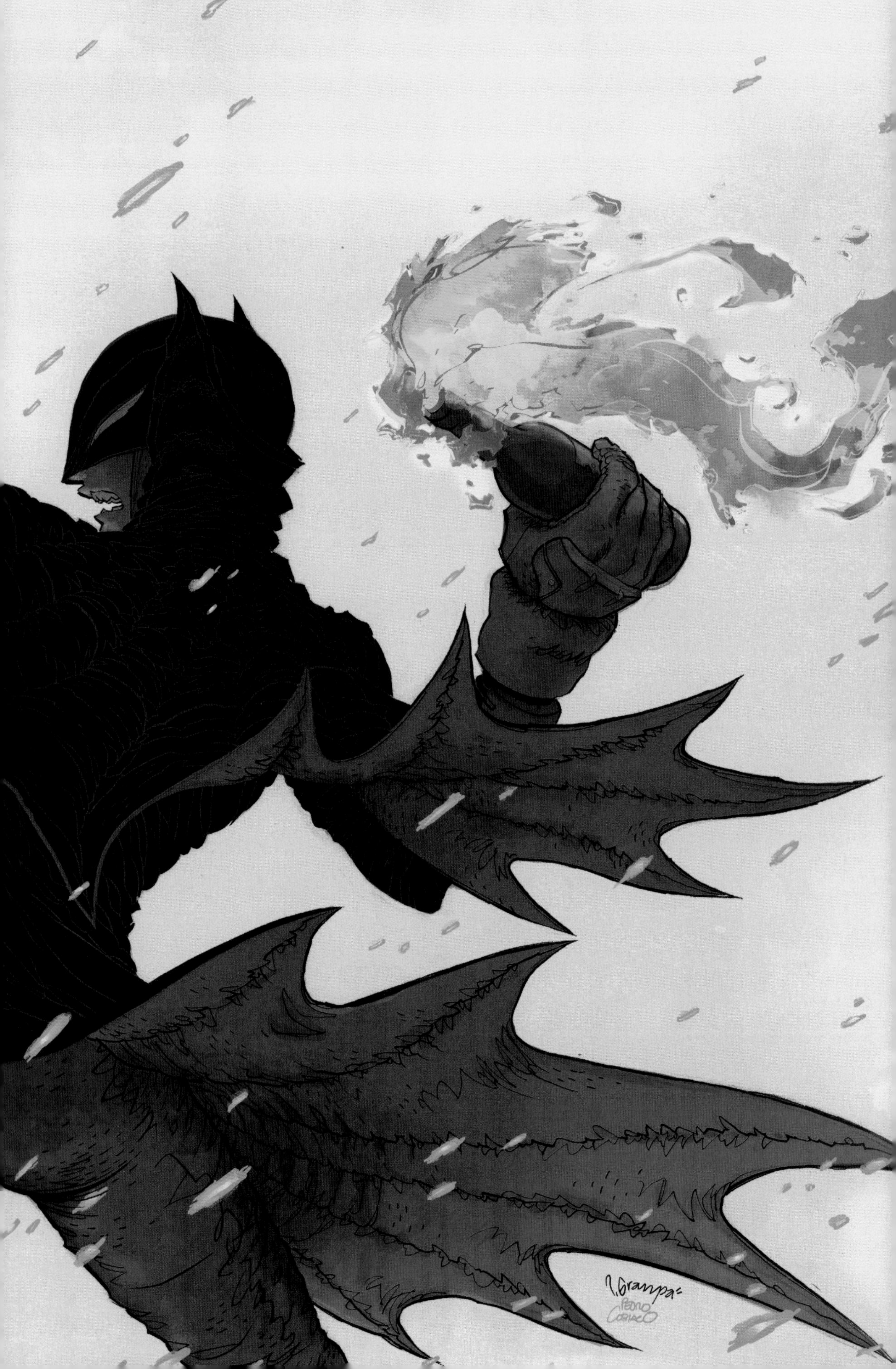

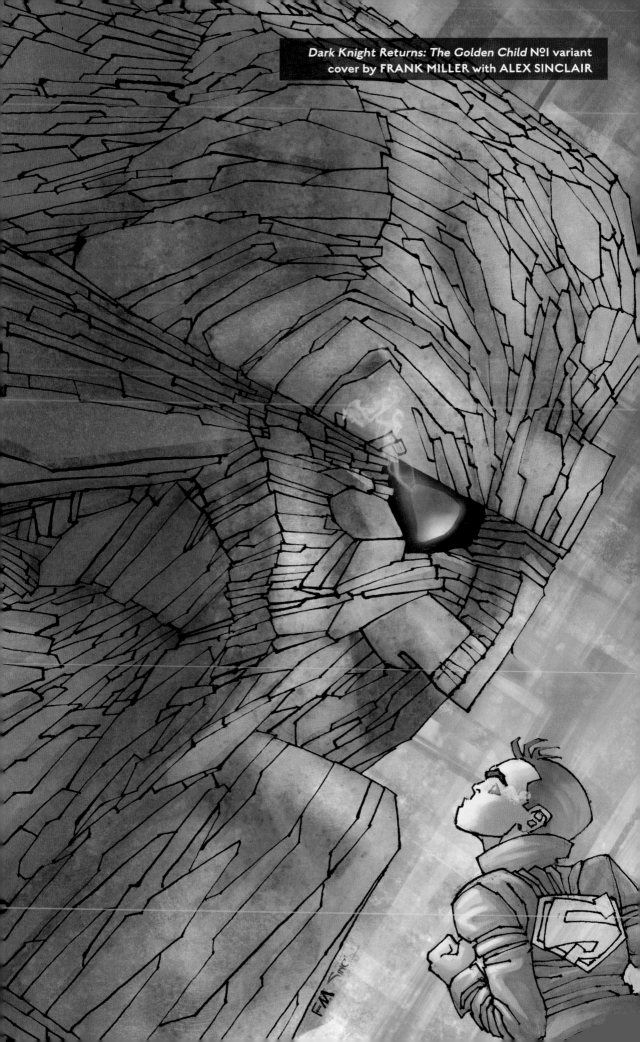

Dark Knight Returns: The Golden Child №1 variant cover by FRANK MILLER with ALEX SINCLAIR

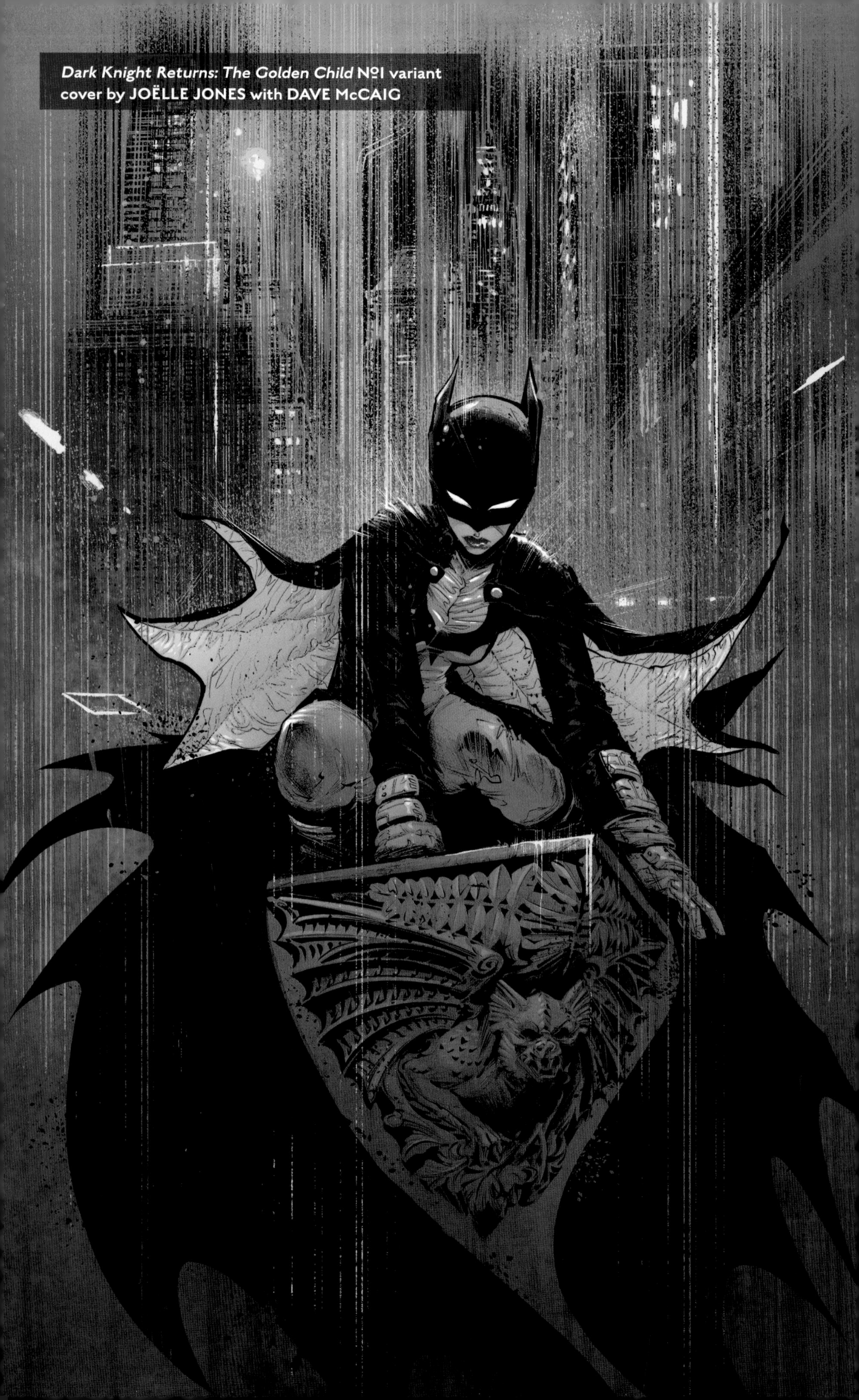

Dark Knight Returns: The Golden Child №1 variant cover by JOËLLE JONES with DAVE McCAIG

Dark Knight Returns: The Golden Child №1 variant
cover by ANDY KUBERT with BRAD ANDERSON

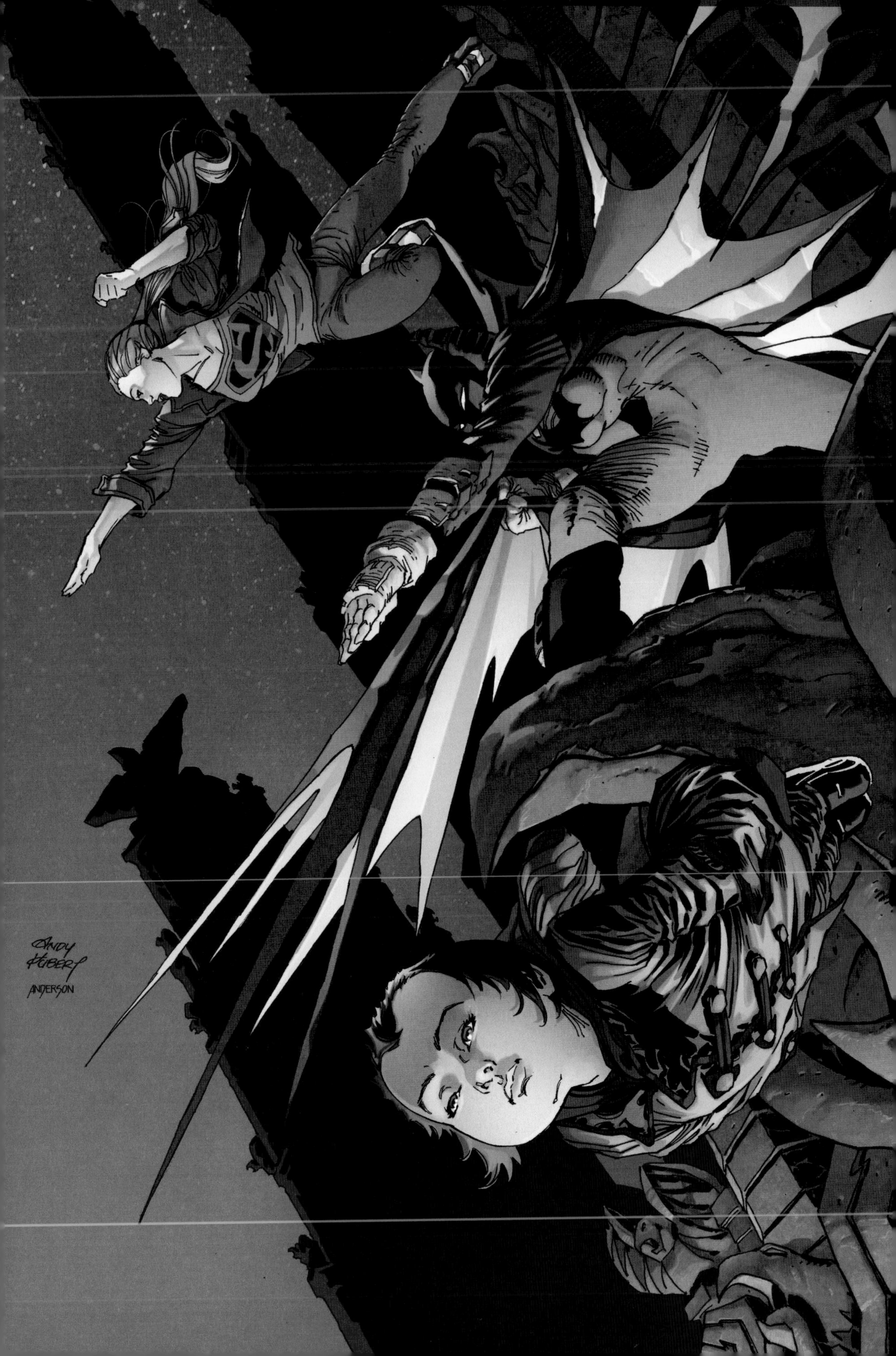

Dark Knight Returns: The Golden Child №1 variant cover by **PAUL POPE** with **JOSÉ VILLARRUBIA**

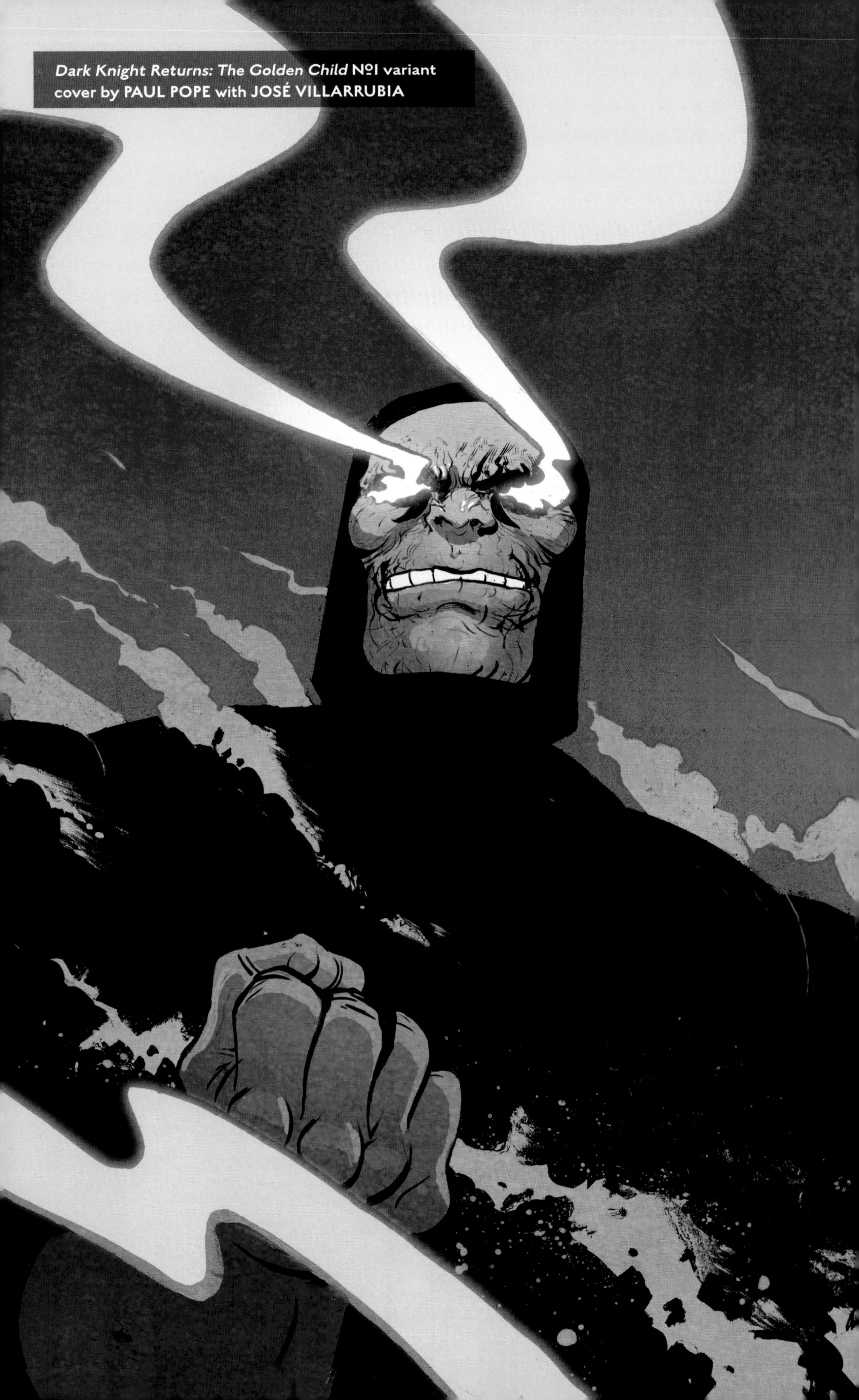

Frank Miller and Rafael Grampá first met in 2015 at an industry dinner in São Paulo. They had golden ants for dinner. For sure, something special was going to happen after such a dinner.

Rafael had admired Frank's work since he was a child and Frank fell in love with Raf's work as soon as he saw it.

In 2016—at Frank's studio in New York—Rafael presented Frank with his version of Batman and Carrie Kelley from his variant cover for *The Dark Knight III: The Master Race*. Frank loved Raf's interpretation of his characters—this was the first seed of a potential collaboration. Frank is often quoted saying, "I'll never draw Carrie the same way again. He topped me."

The pair began to organically explore what a Frank Miller-Rafael Grampá collaboration could look like...

Eventually, a new addition to the *Dark Knight Returns* universe was envisioned.

The Golden Child was authored by Frank Miller in dialogue with Rafael Grampá as an opportunity to explore the next generation of superheroes: the children of Superman and Wonder Woman—Jonathan and Lara Kent with Carrie Kelley as Batwoman. Frank and Rafael also wanted to provide a satirical commentary on the political circumstance of our times as context. They understood they needed a superhero riot story.

Over several months, in many cities around the world (New York, Los Angeles, Amsterdam, Paris, London, São Paulo) Frank and Rafael brainstormed the key elements of this new saga and its characters. Once these elements were assembled, the conversations about characters, story, and universe were fleshed out, and the first references, sketches, and characters were developed in 2017.

As a big fan of Frank and the *DKR* saga, and with his background in art direction, Rafael knew he needed to evoke Frank's art in his work to maintain the legacy and respect the look of the epic saga. Raf started to experiment with a way to mix some of Frank's techniques with his own style, with the goal of giving the fans a real *DKR* book.

Out of this collaboration, Frank wrote the plot summary for *The Golden Child* and Rafael developed the thumbnails in 2018.

Beginning in 2019, Rafael developed the pencils and inks for 48 pages—meeting with Frank in stages to discuss batches of pages and how they related to the story, as well as important plot details and any next steps. Frank gave Rafael a level of freedom to create the character designs and to elaborate on the scenes of the story in ways he wasn't expecting.

Upon Rafael finishing all the inks in September 2019, Frank finalized the script and dialogue.

At the same time that this was happening, Rafael and Frank developed their color references as a guide for artist Jordie Bellaire in her interpretation of the work.

Collectively the trio agreed on an approach—with the idea of using the page gutters' colors as mood indicators for the scenes—and Jordie brought her unique POV to the project.

The rest is history and you now hold the results in your hands.

Enjoy the ride.

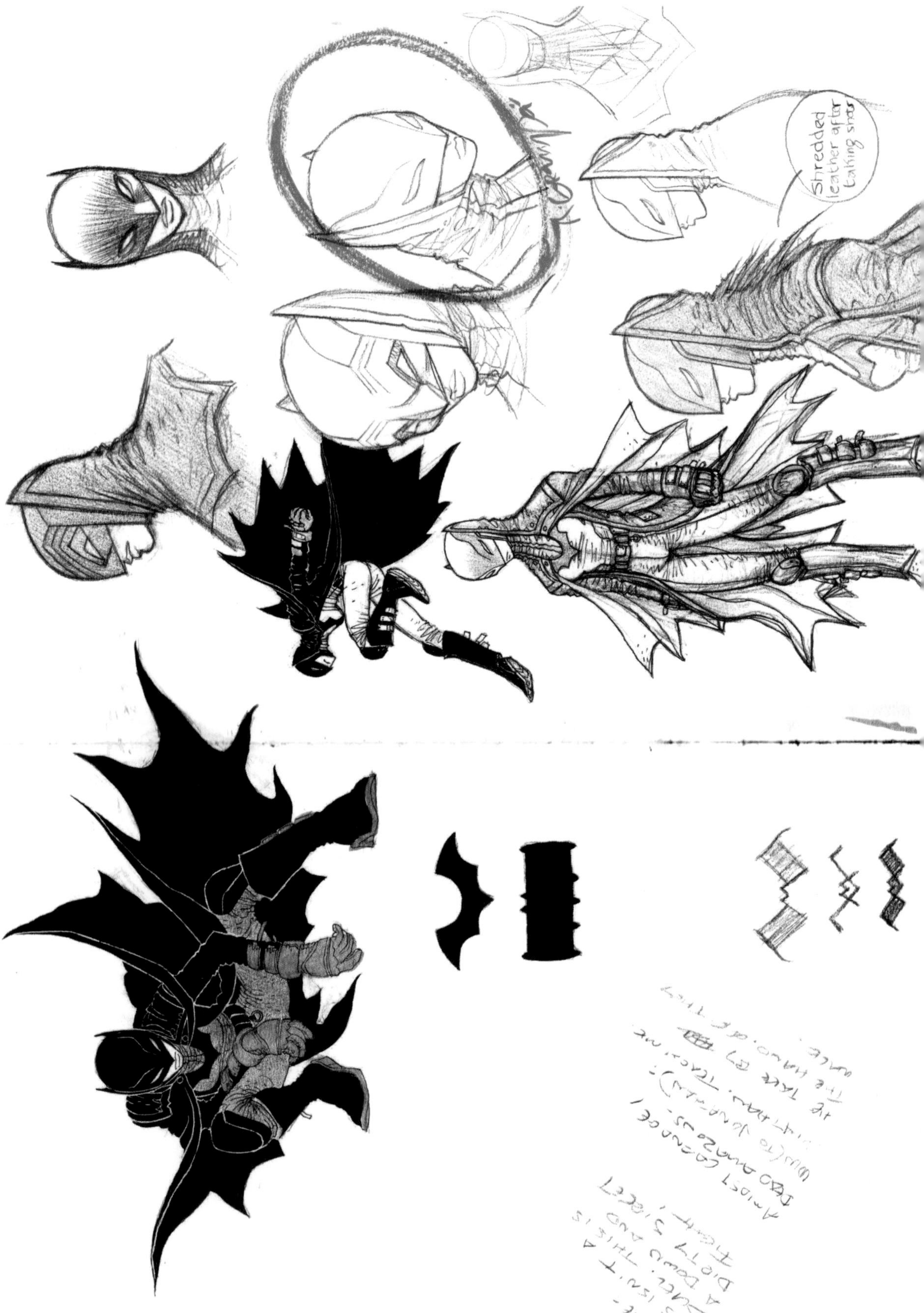
Shredded leather after taking shots

*All images and sketchbook commentary by **Rafael Grampá***

This is not the first time I drew Carrie's design, but it's a version where I figured out the final version of the costume design (only modifying by taking the belt off). The pose where Carrie is crouching is inspired by a drawing by Russian artist Yaroslav Astapeev.

In this image, I was starting to mix Frank's style with mine, to see if it worked. This was the first sketch of Carrie that Frank saw.

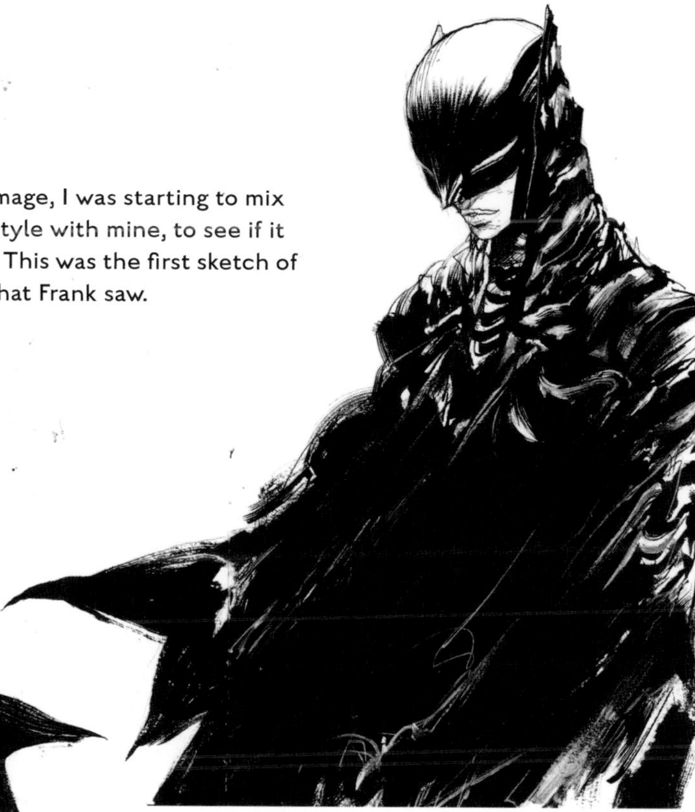

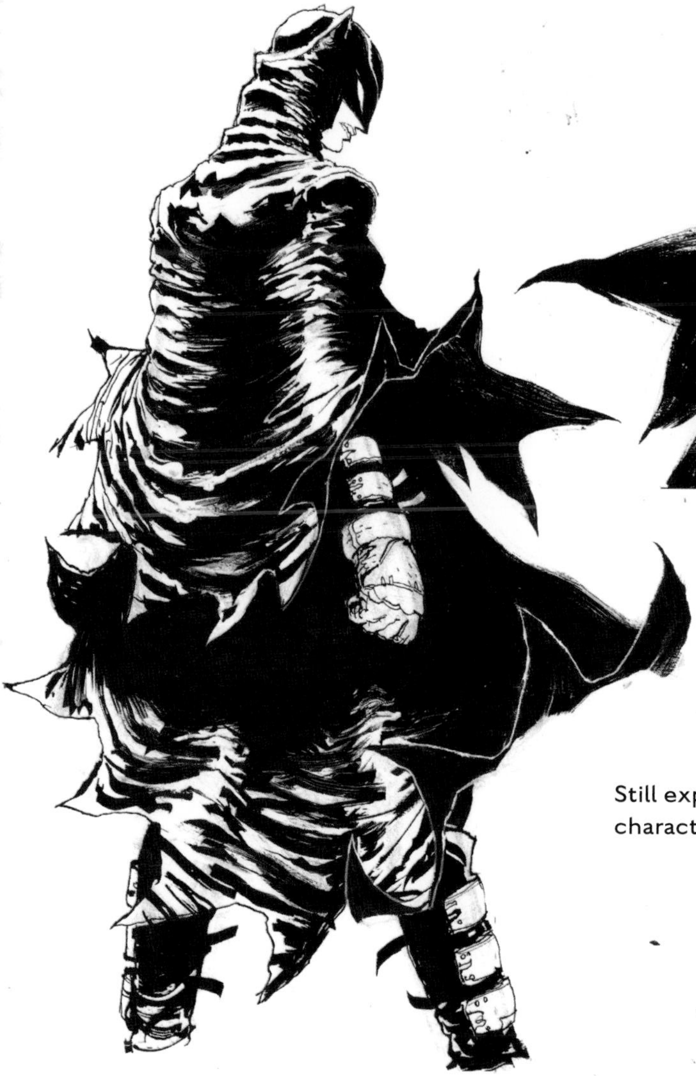

Still experimenting with the character and inking technique.

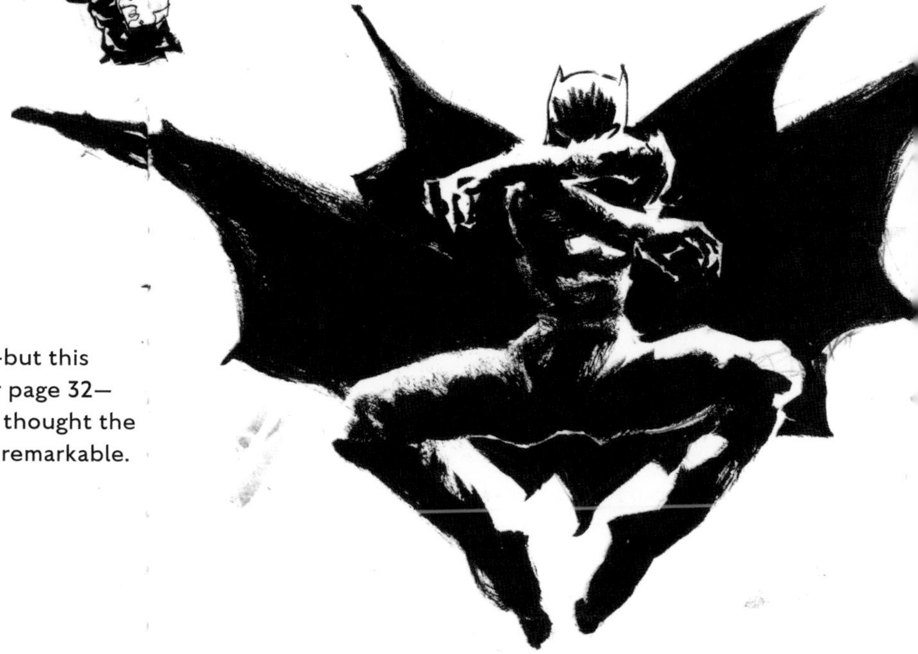

Still experimenting—but this became the pose for page 32—the jumping scene. I thought the silhouette would be remarkable.

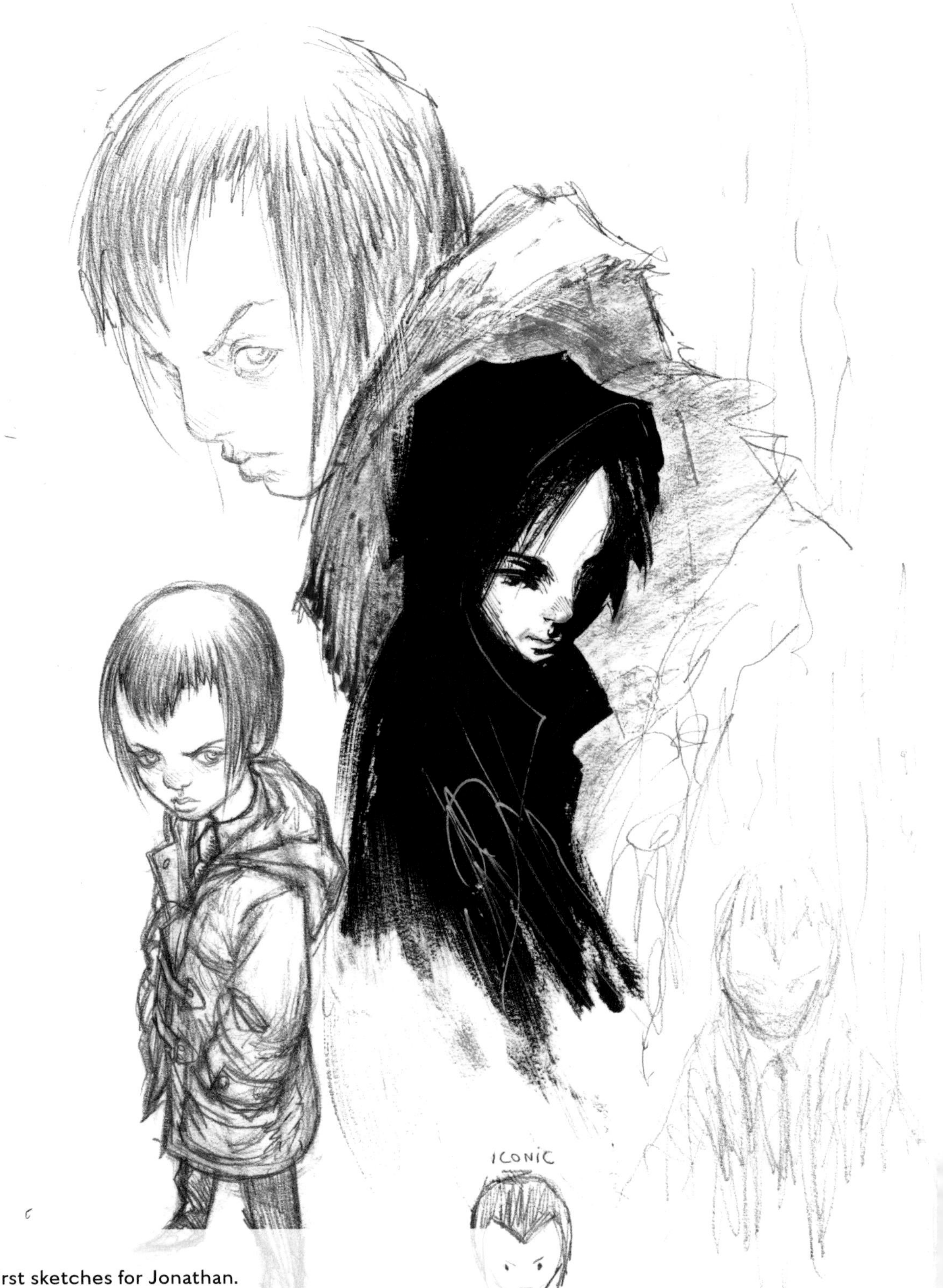

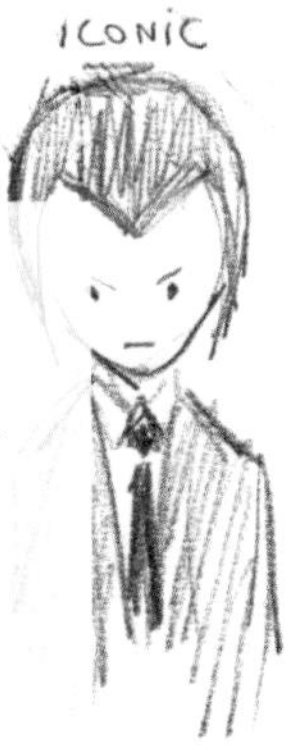
ICONIC

First sketches for Jonathan.

When I create a character it needs to first work only as a silhouette with iconic elements. If it works like this, I know it will work in other forms.

With Jonathan, I tried to create an iconic haircut in a way—you can recognize him even if he is an emoji...

I also wanted him to have a very serious adult mood and a very arrogant expression. He accidentally ended up looking like Liam Gallagher.

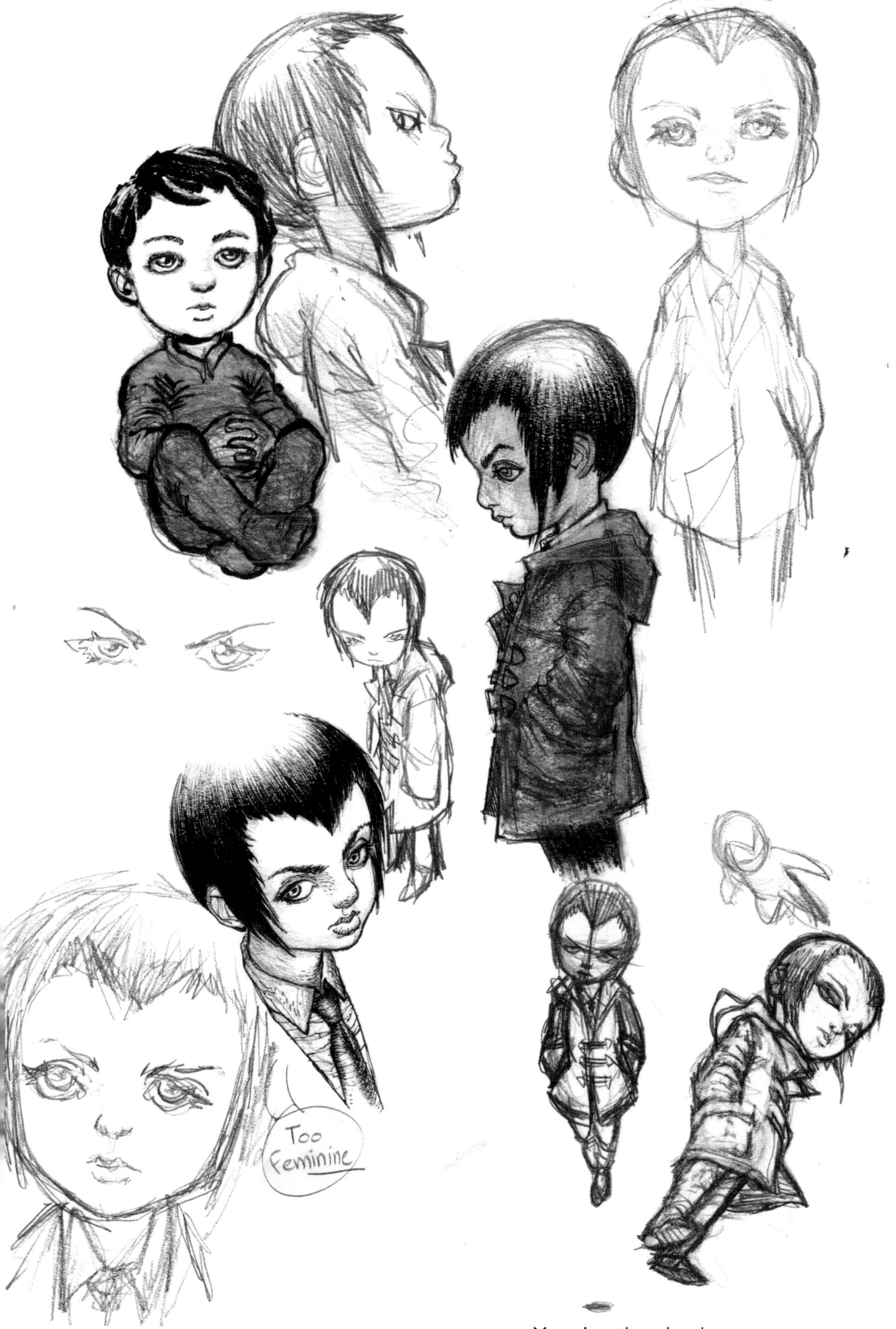
Too
Feminine

More Jonathan sketches.

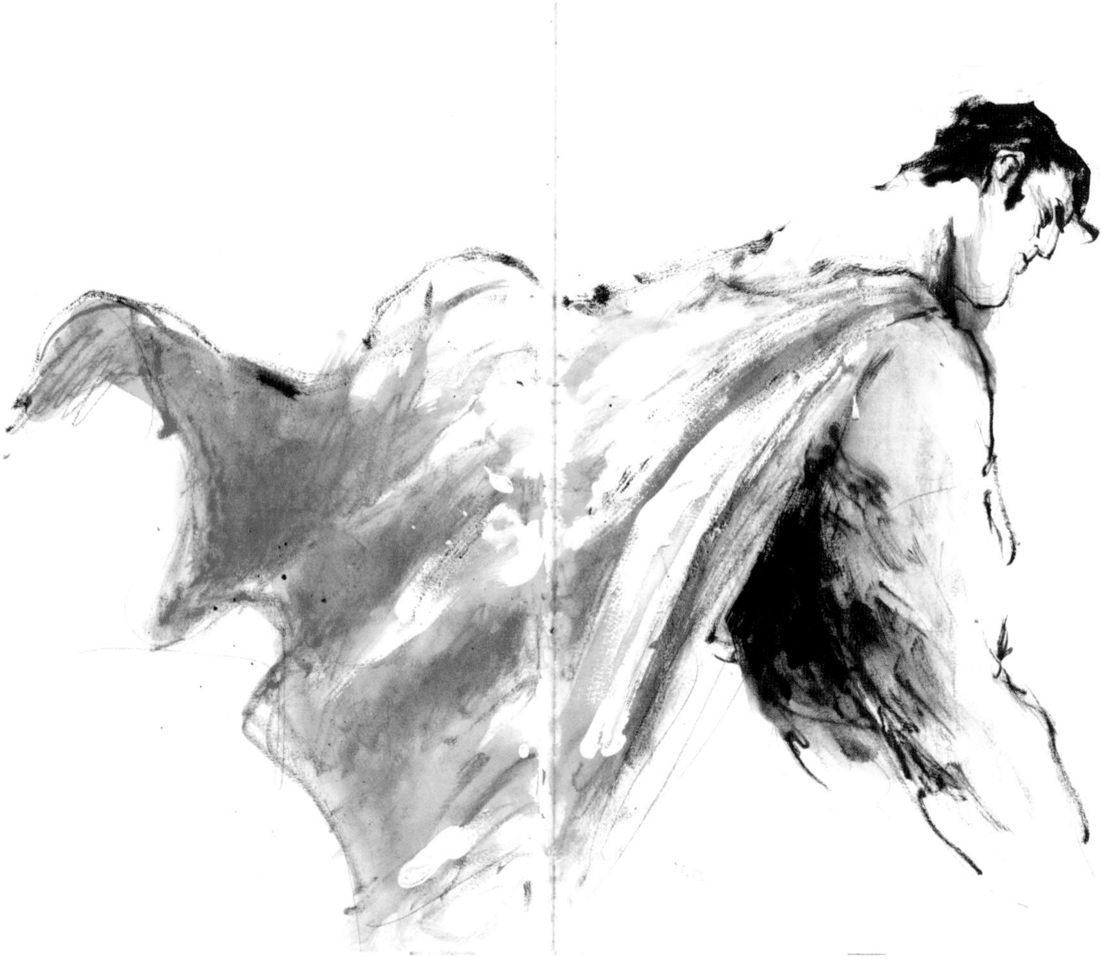

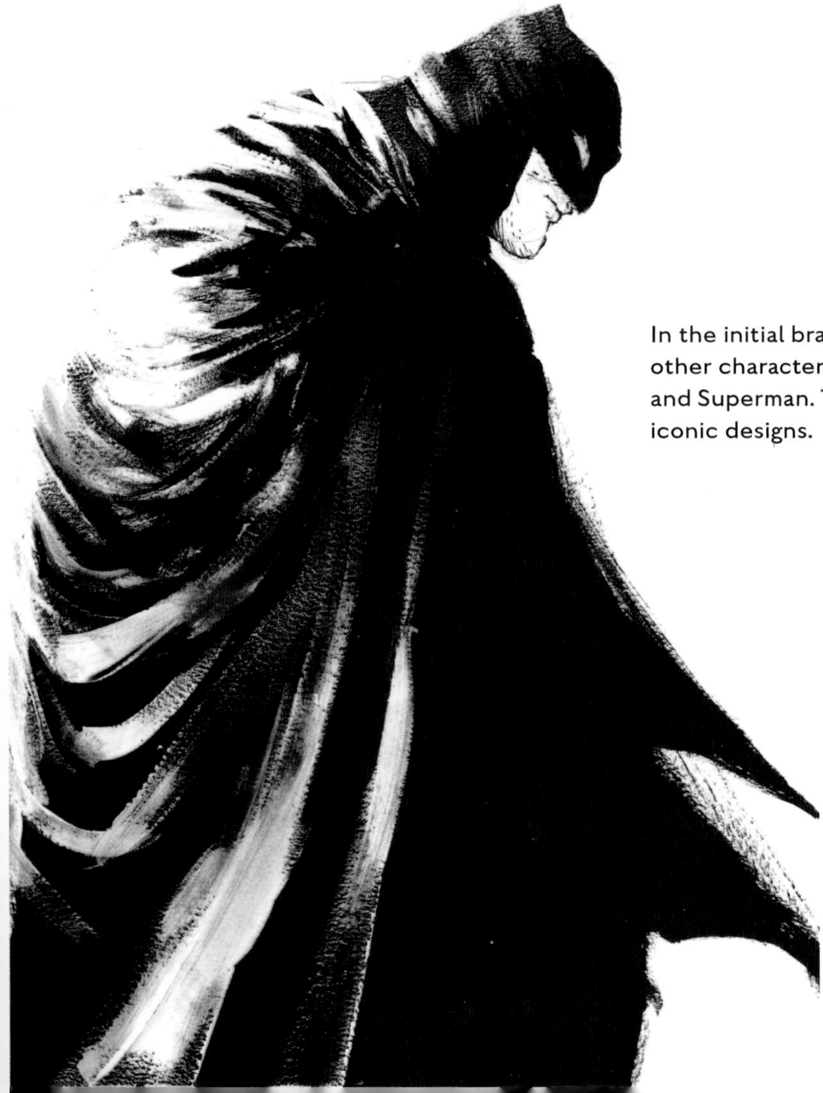

In the initial brainstorming, we explored using other characters. These are tests for Batman and Superman. They are my versions of Frank's iconic designs.

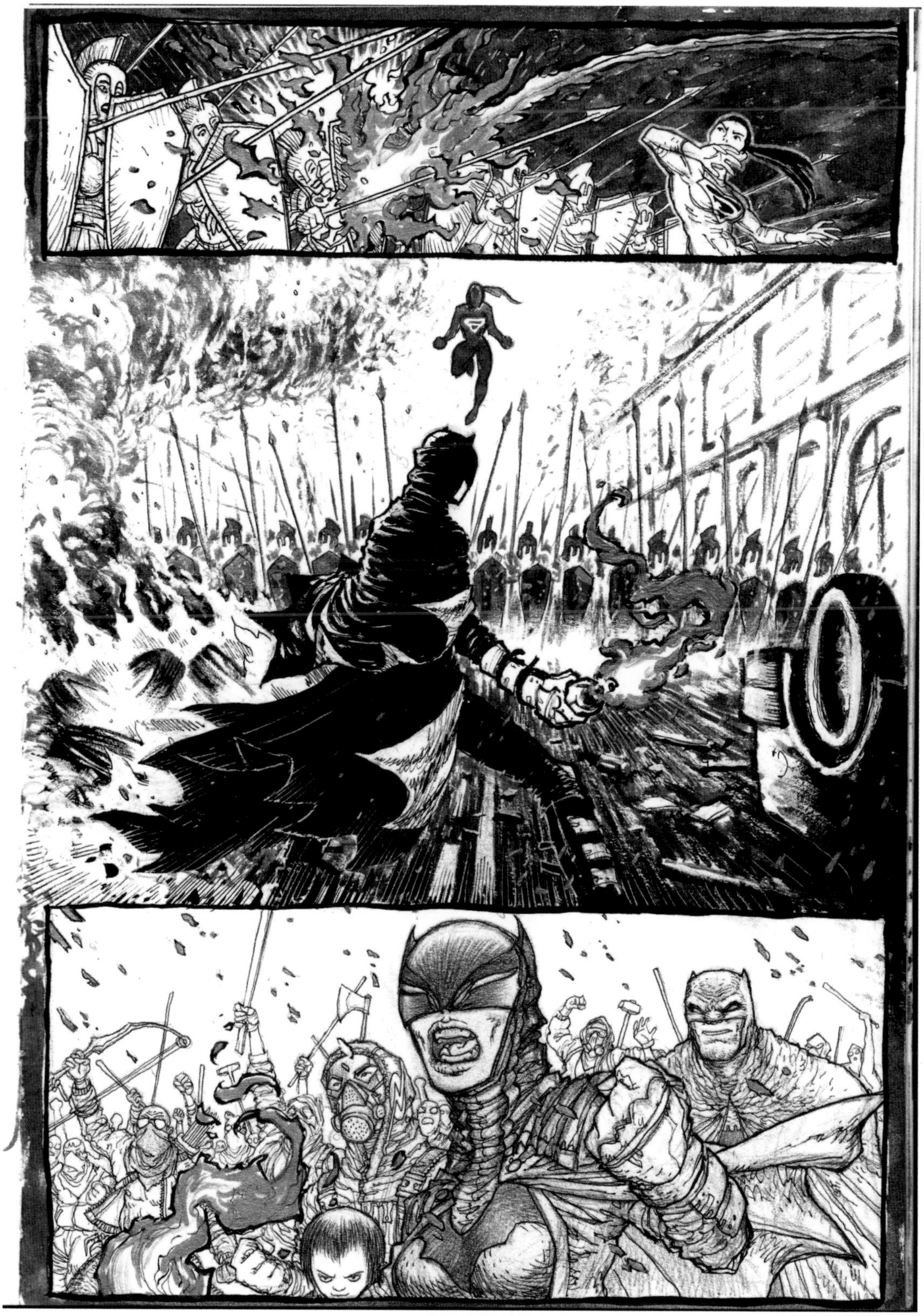

This is the most important sketch of all, because this was the key foundational concept proposed to Frank after initial plot discussions. This is a pivotal scene in the story, which the rest of the story is built upon. This scene was originally planned to be a fight between the Amazons and the superheroes.

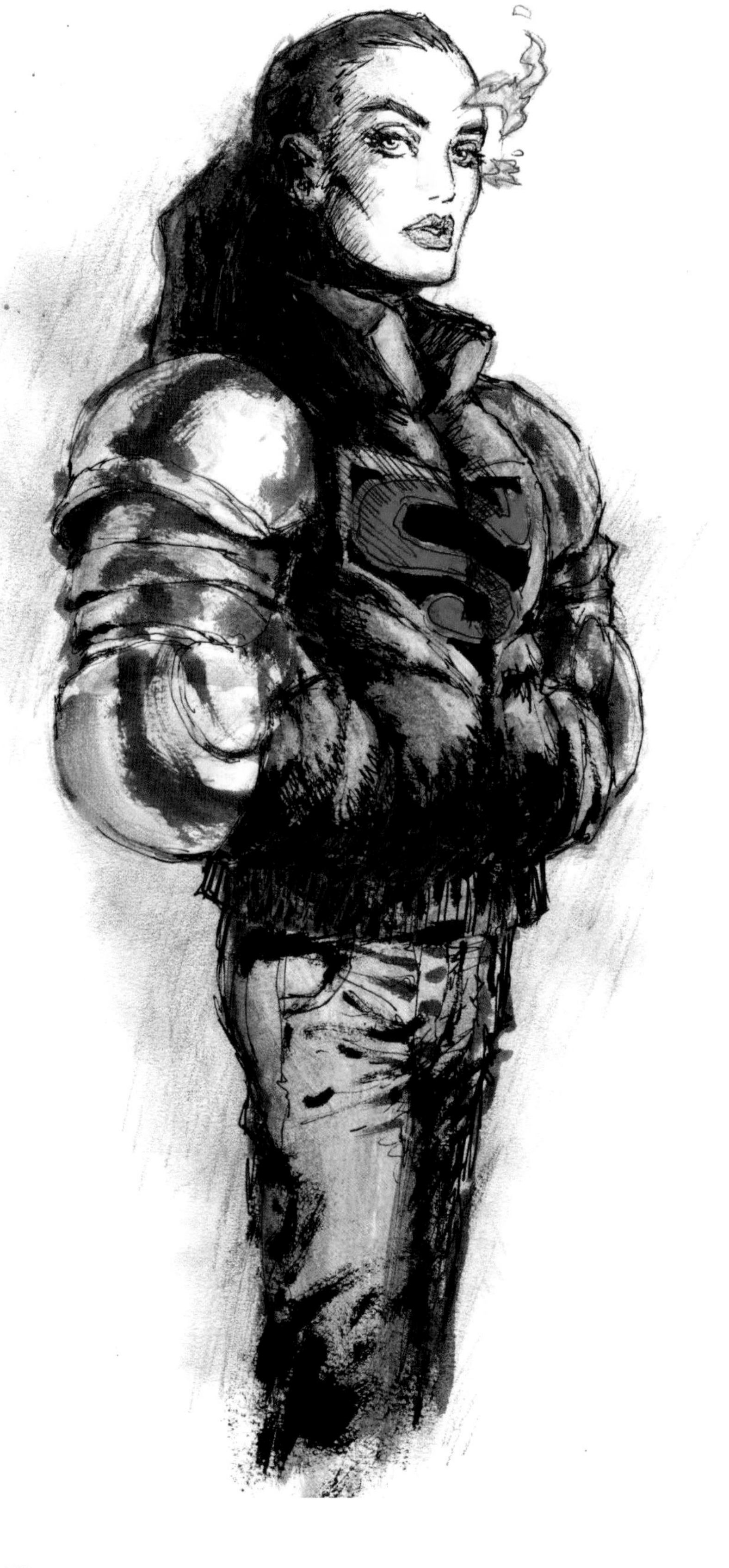

First idea for Lara.

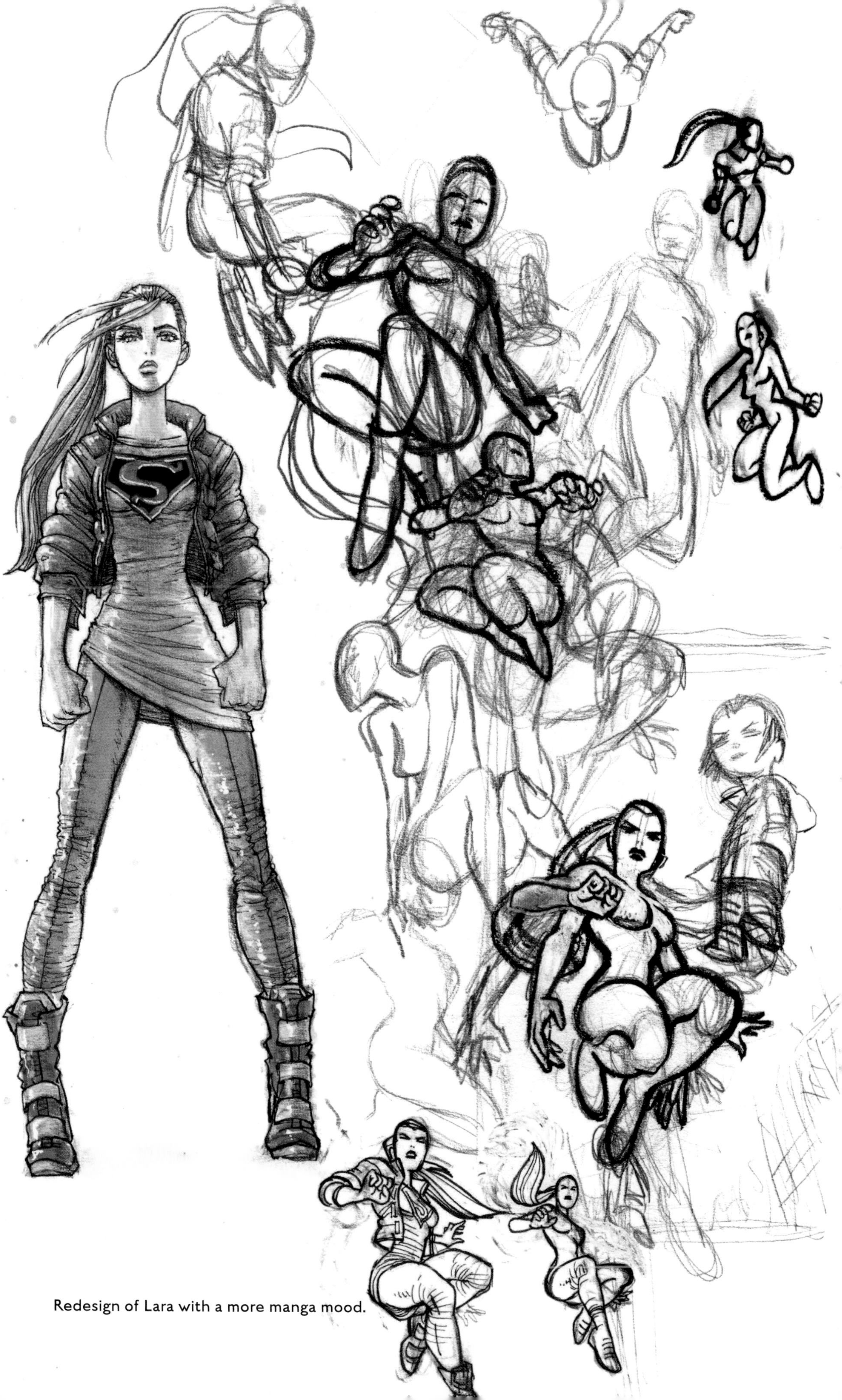

Redesign of Lara with a more manga mood.

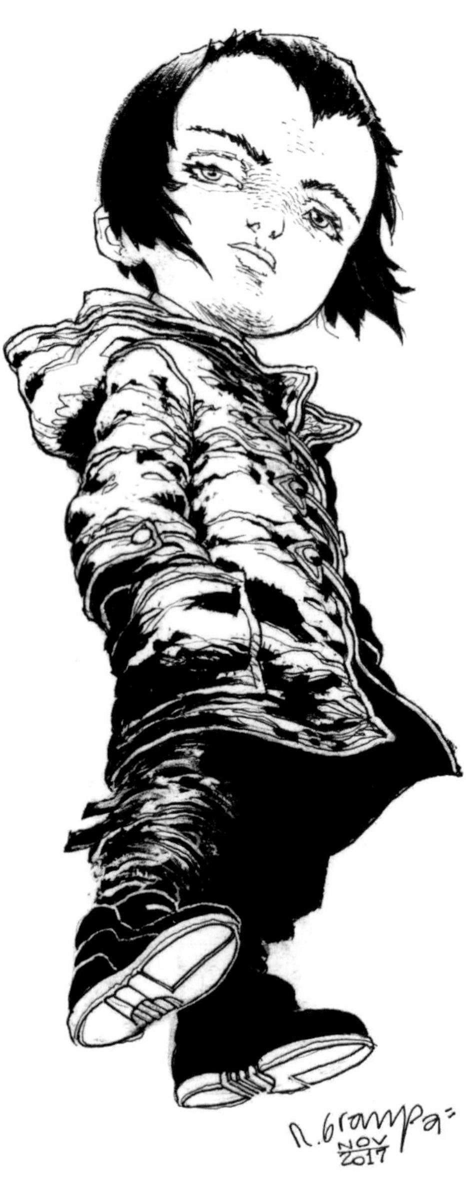
NOV
2017

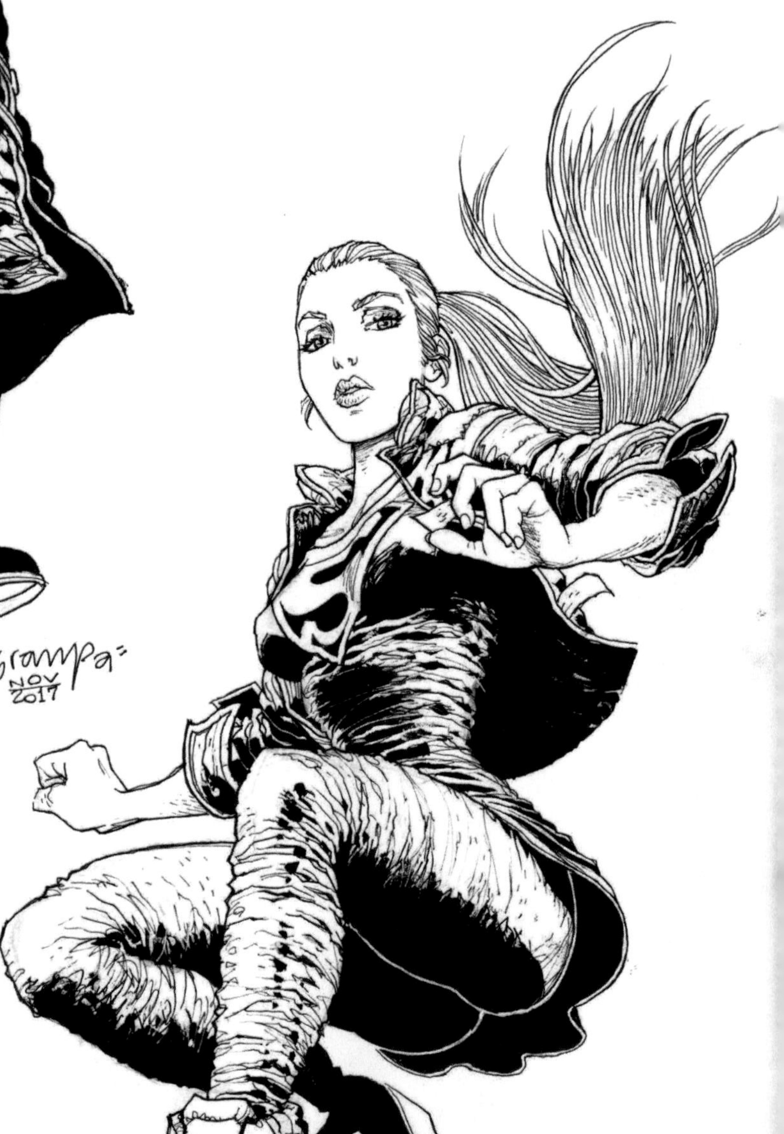
NOV
2017

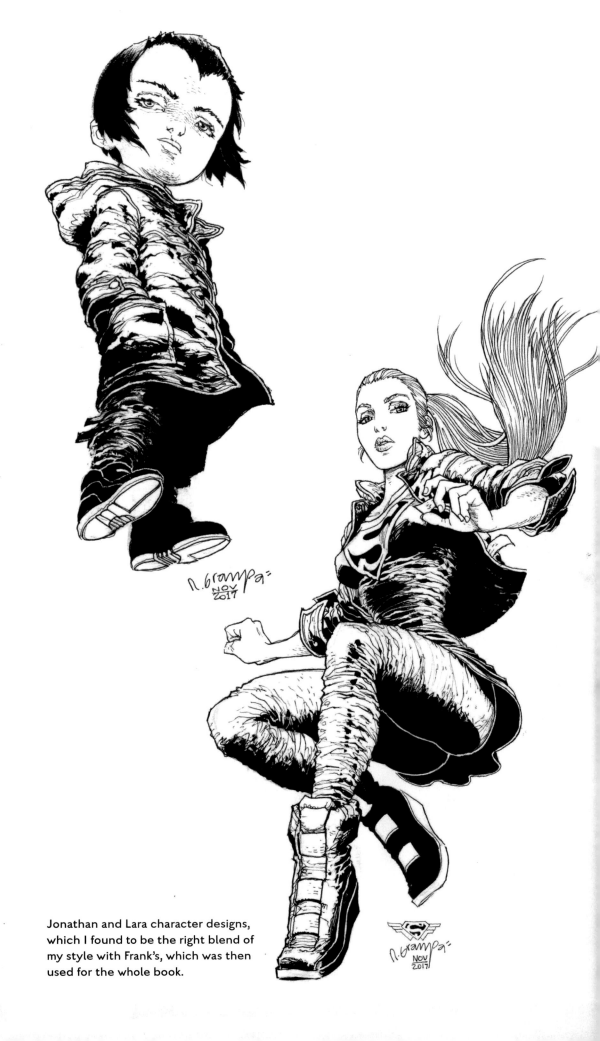

Jonathan and Lara character designs, which I found to be the right blend of my style with Frank's, which was then used for the whole book.

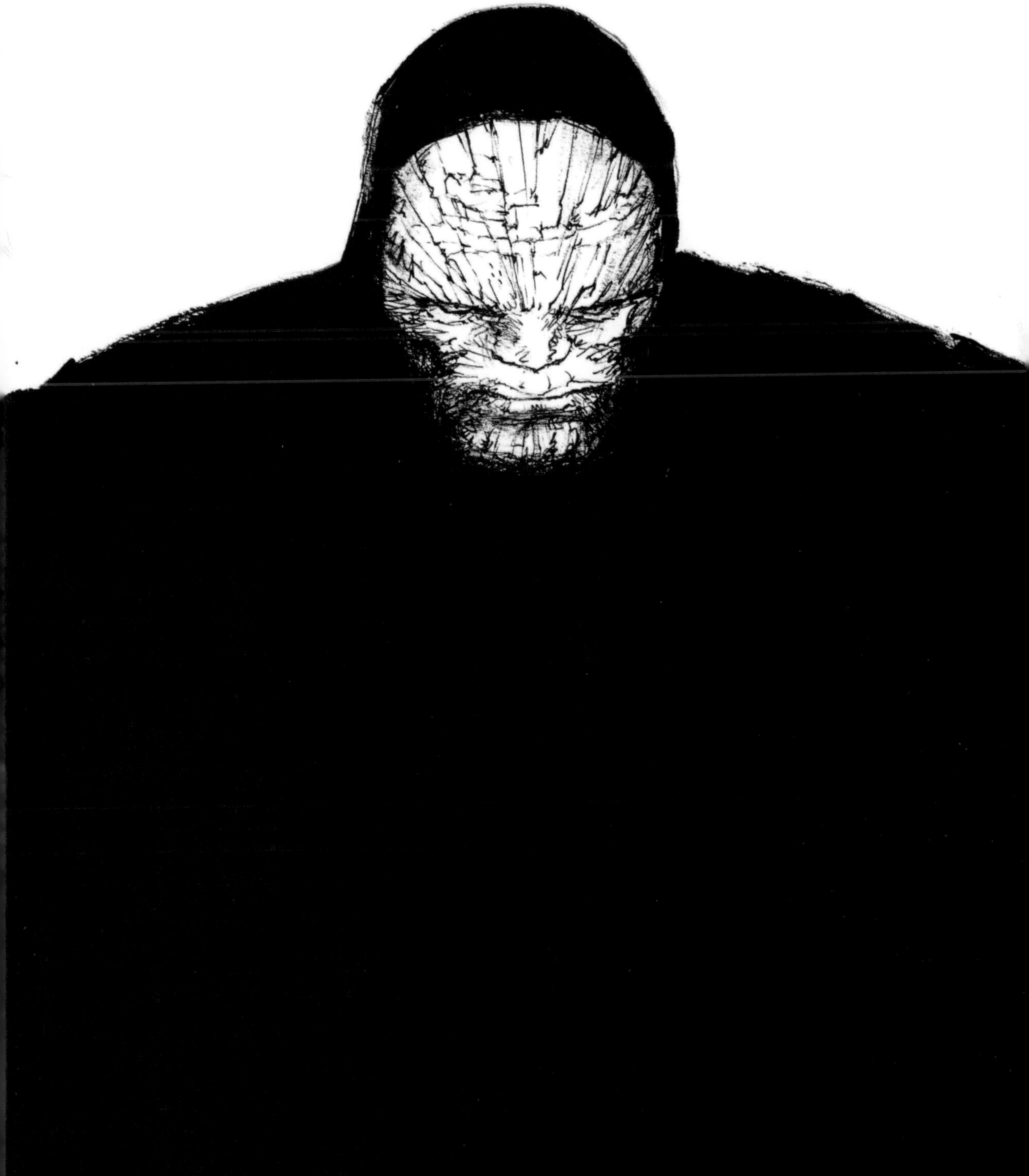

Concept design for Darkseid—dark coloring because of the name...I created a Darker Seid.

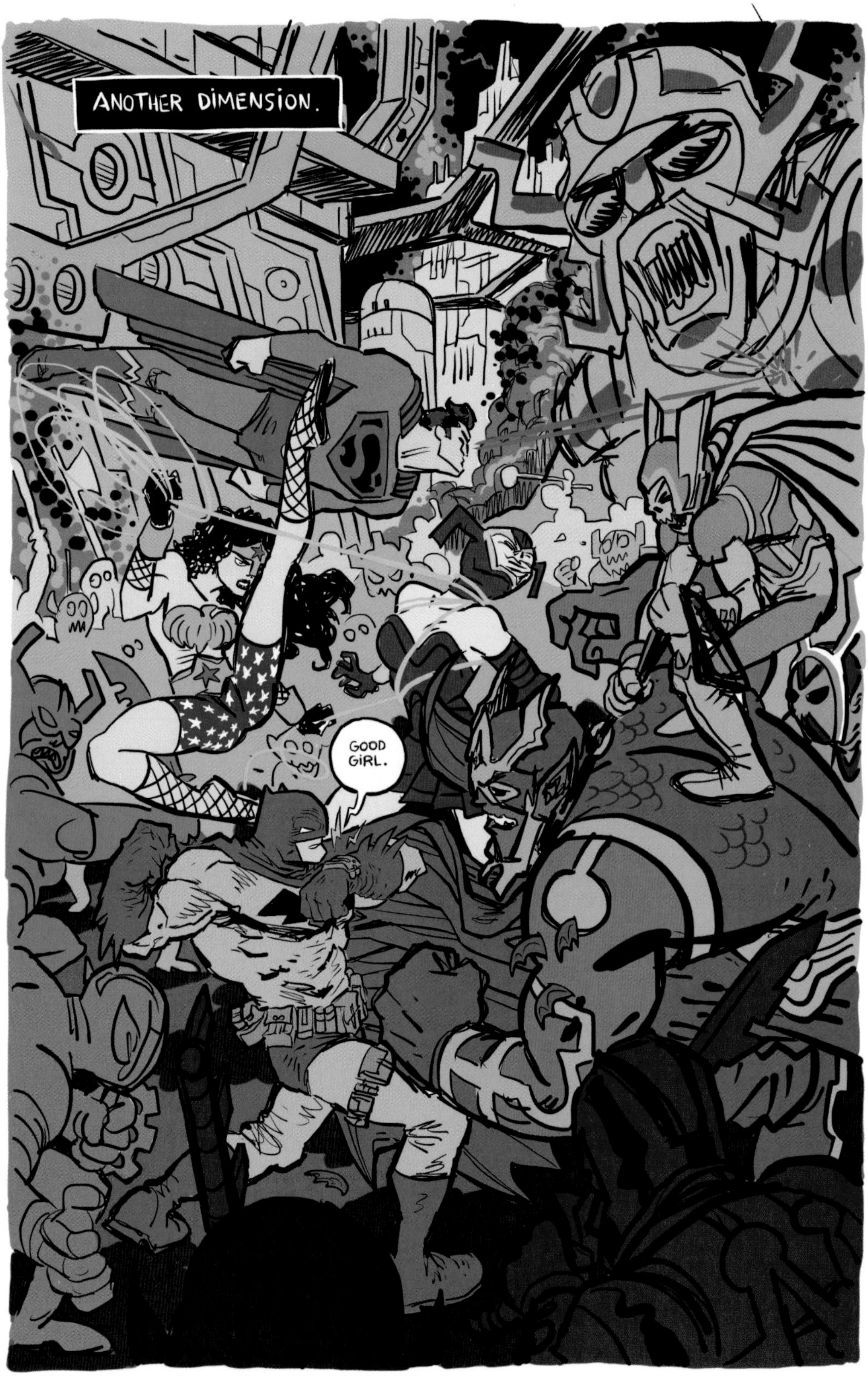
ANOTHER DIMENSION.
GOOD GIRL.

Another dimension: Batman calling Carrie Kelley to respond to her "Clown Down" message. Instead, we went with Carrie using the Bat app/emojis in the final version to show the teenage nature of Carrie—which is more original and fun.

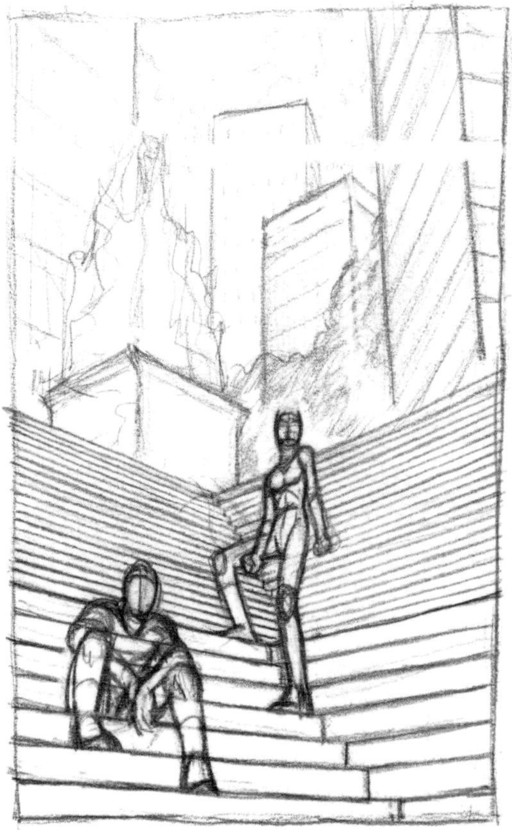

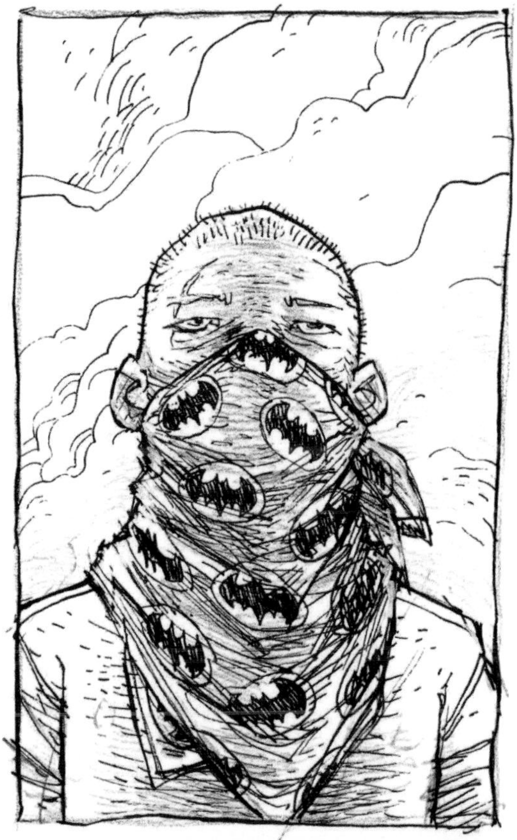

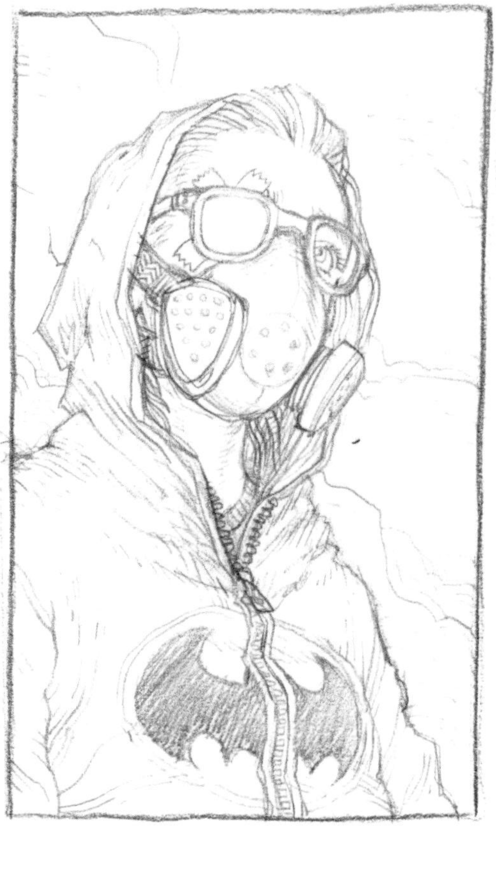

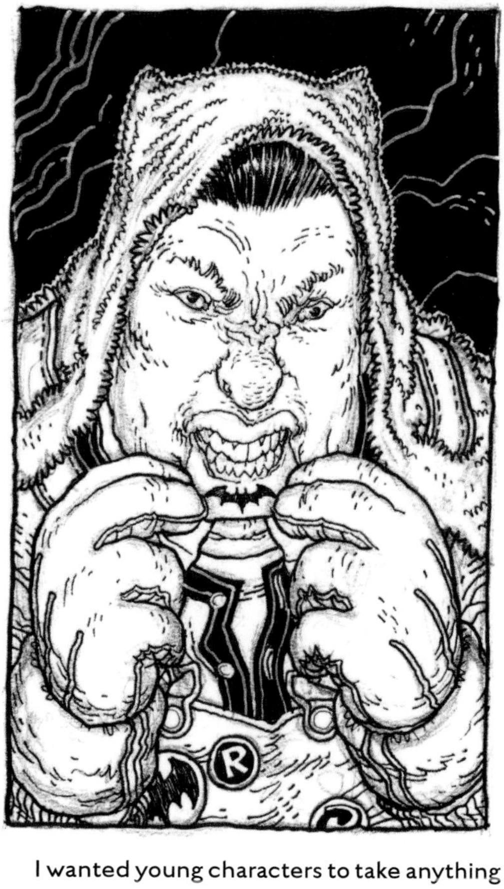

I wanted young characters to take anything they could find with the Bat symbol...that they could make a costume out of.

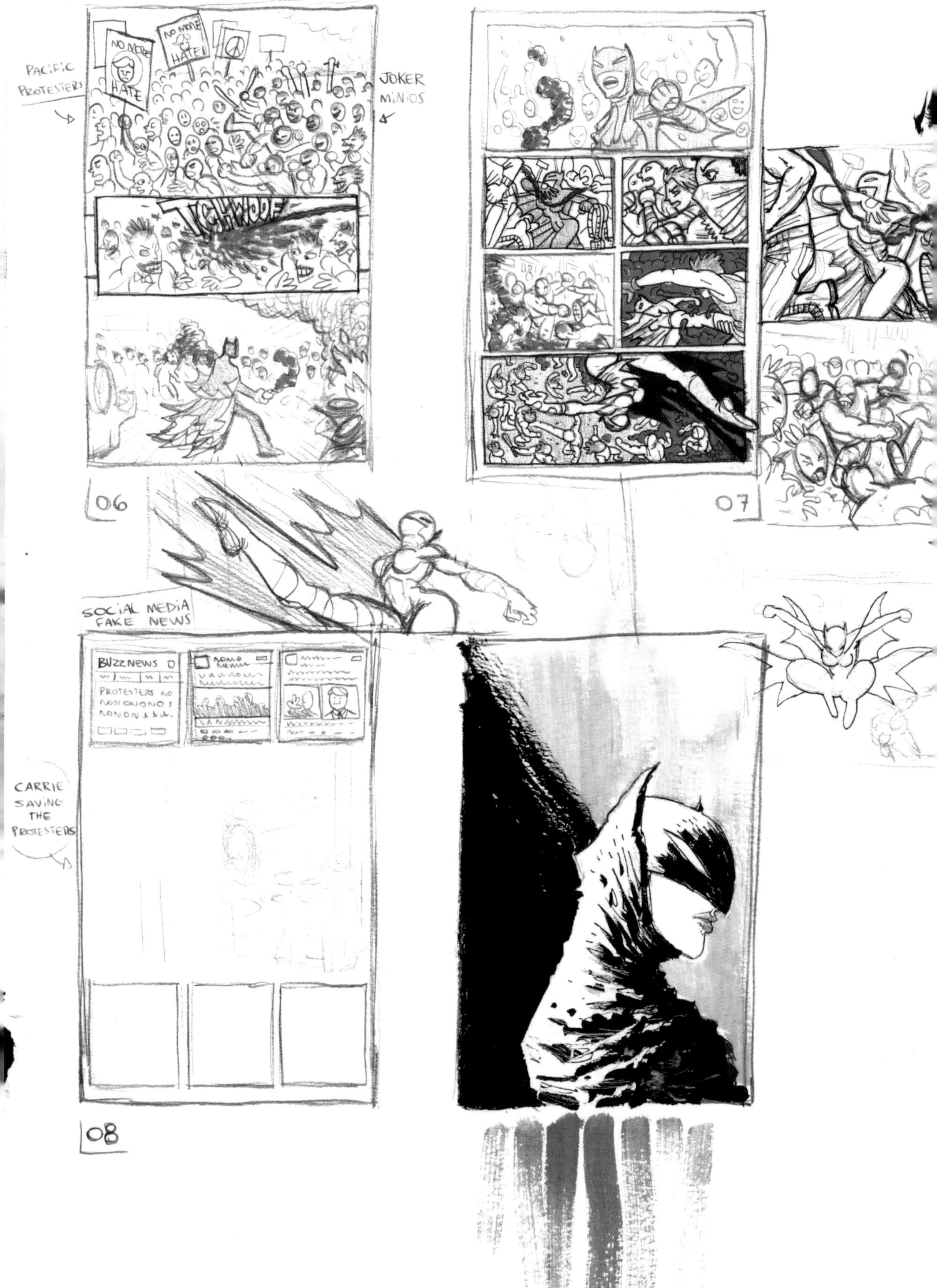

PACIFIC PROTESTERS
NO MORE HATE
NO MORE HATE
JOKER MINIOS
06
07
SOCIAL MEDIA FAKE NEWS
BUZZNEWS
CARRIE SAVING THE PROTESTERS
08

Early storyboards on paper—before the process was moved to digital for the sake of speed.

LARA JON

cific TESTERS

JOKER MINIONS

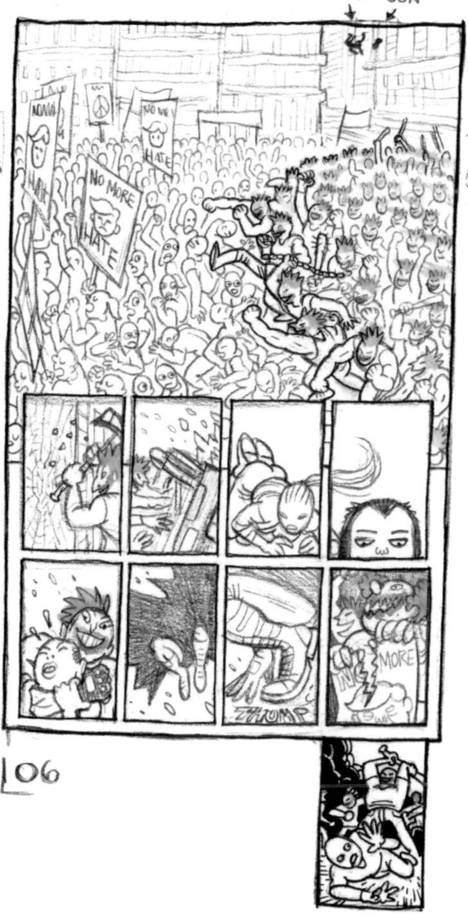
NO MORE HATE
THUMP

06

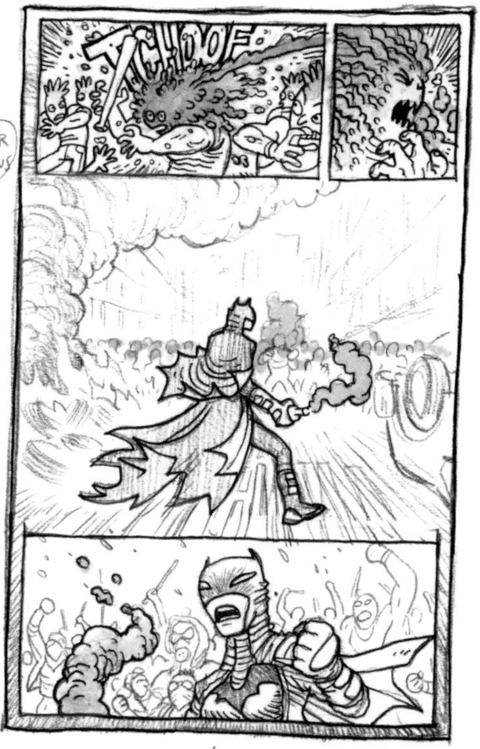
TCHOOF!

07

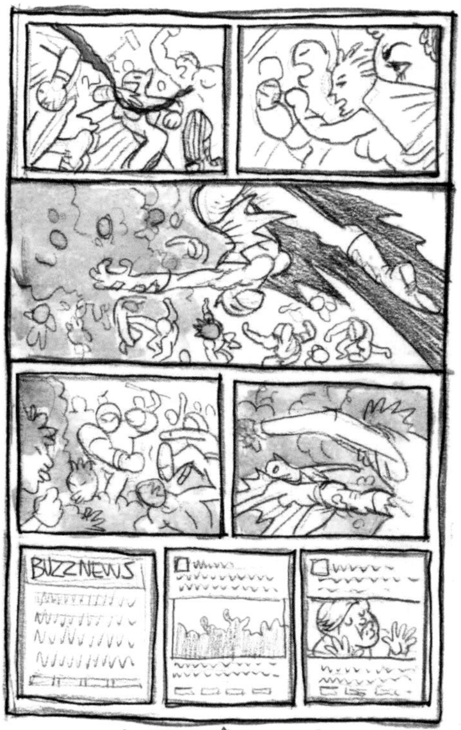
BUZZ NEWS

08

Fake News

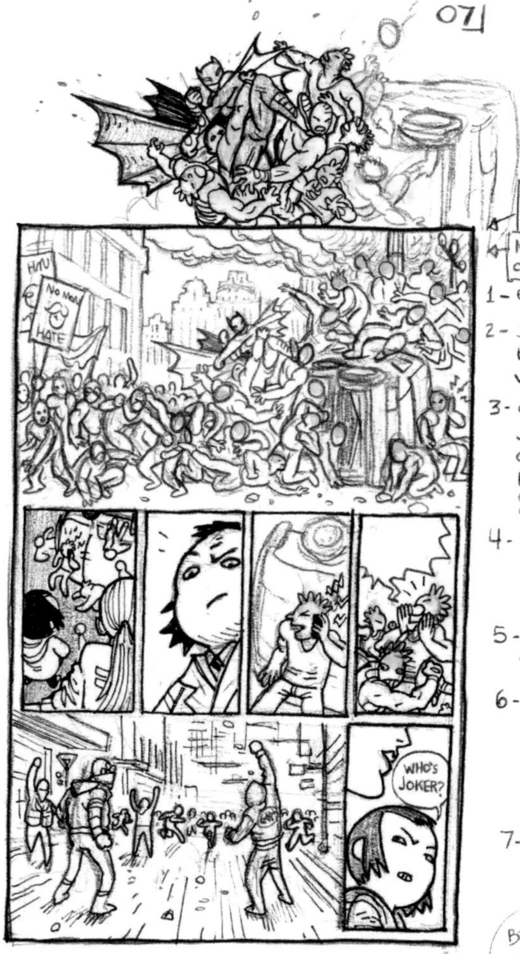
NO MORE HATE
WHO'S JOKER?

09

Let's make this panel in a full page?

Maybe turn it into a duble page?

1 - epic batlle

2 - Joker minion on the phone. Jon watch him.

3 - close on the Joker minion. In the other side of the phone, somebody give him orders.

4 - Jon listen to the conversation with his super hearing.

5 - The minion says "OK, boss".

6 - The minion spread the order saying: "Joker sayd to Get out! spread the order".

7 - Jon: Who's Joker?

Boss is happy! Time to get out!!

- Joker minions running away in the backeround.

- Batwoman gang celebrating the victory in the foreground.

Above and opposite top:
Portraits of the gang featuring late 1970s–1980s gang style
inspired by movies like *The Warriors* and Michael Jackson's
music video for "Bad."

Opposite bottom:
Sketches for Joker's gang—I wanted each individual to look
different...and I reused them throughout the entire story.

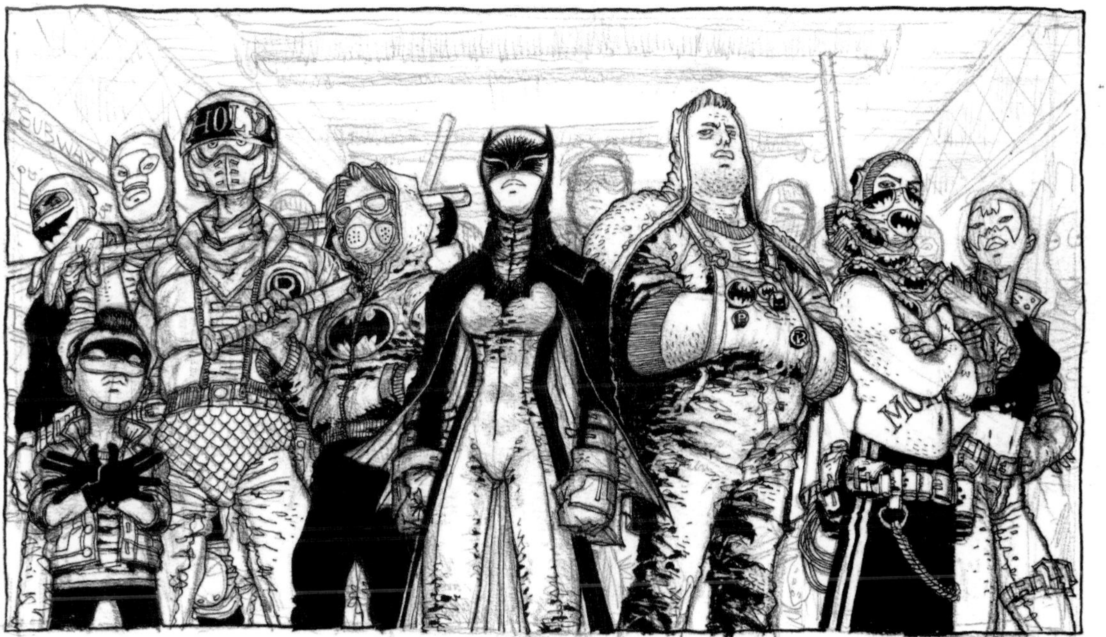
SUBWAY
HOLY

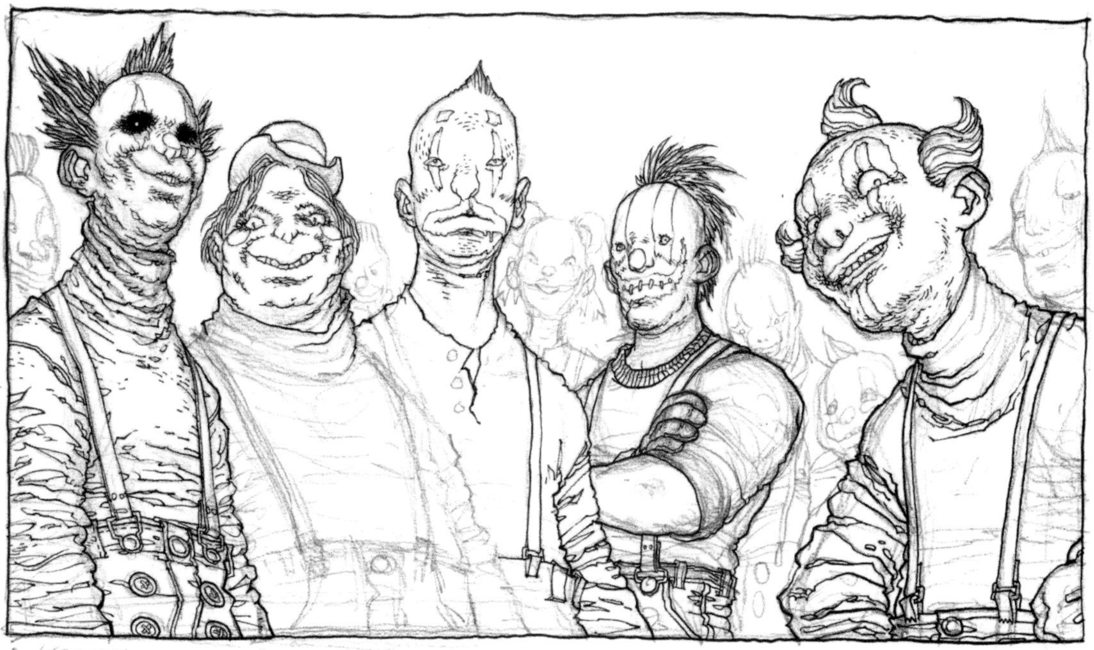

As Frank didn't want any explanation for how/why Joker
is alive again, I decided to make him look like he had
undergone plastic surgery on his face since the last time we
saw him in the Dark Knight saga, where he was burnt!

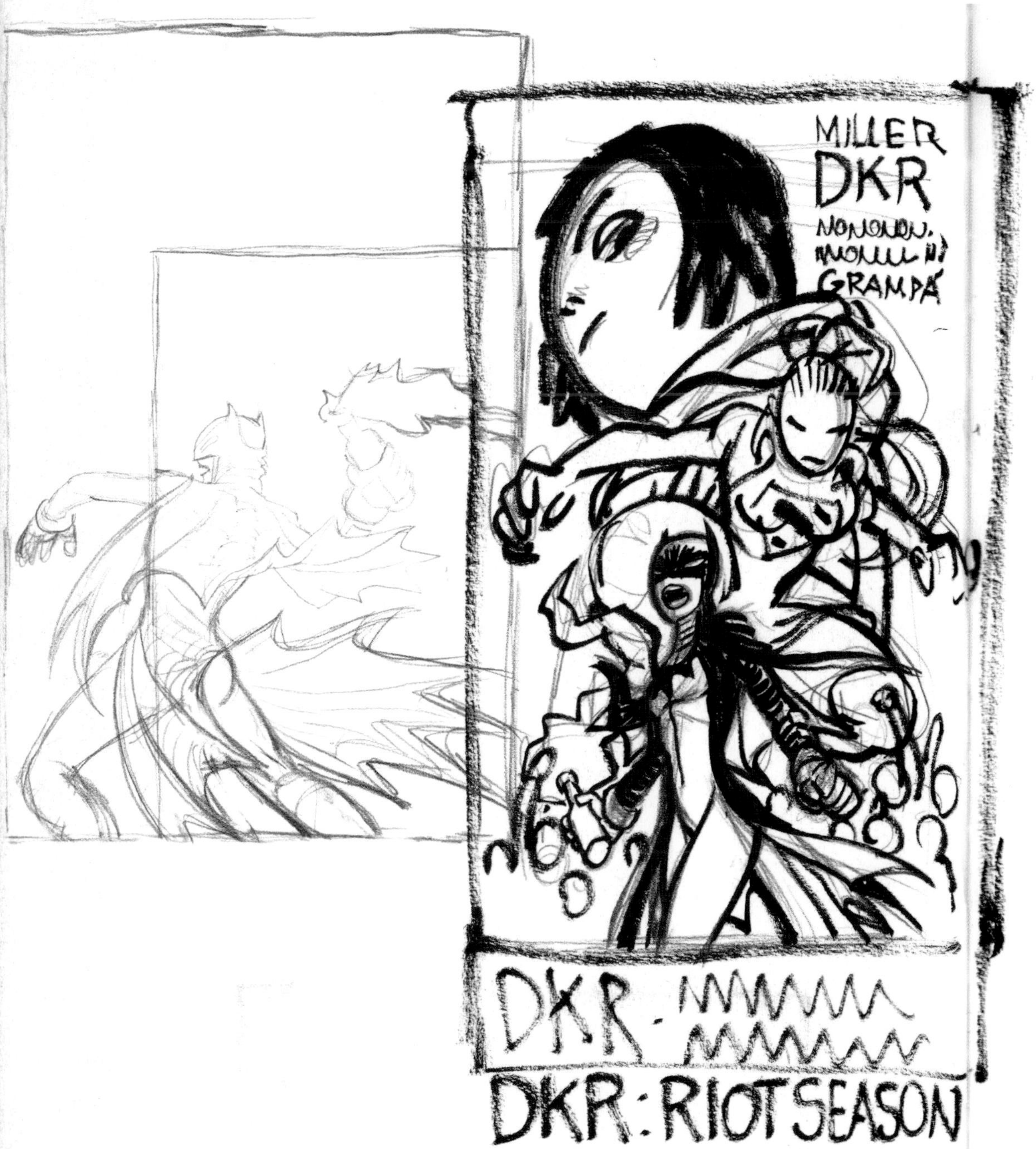
MILLER
DKR
GRAMPA
DKR
DKR: RIOT SEASON

Sketches for my two covers.

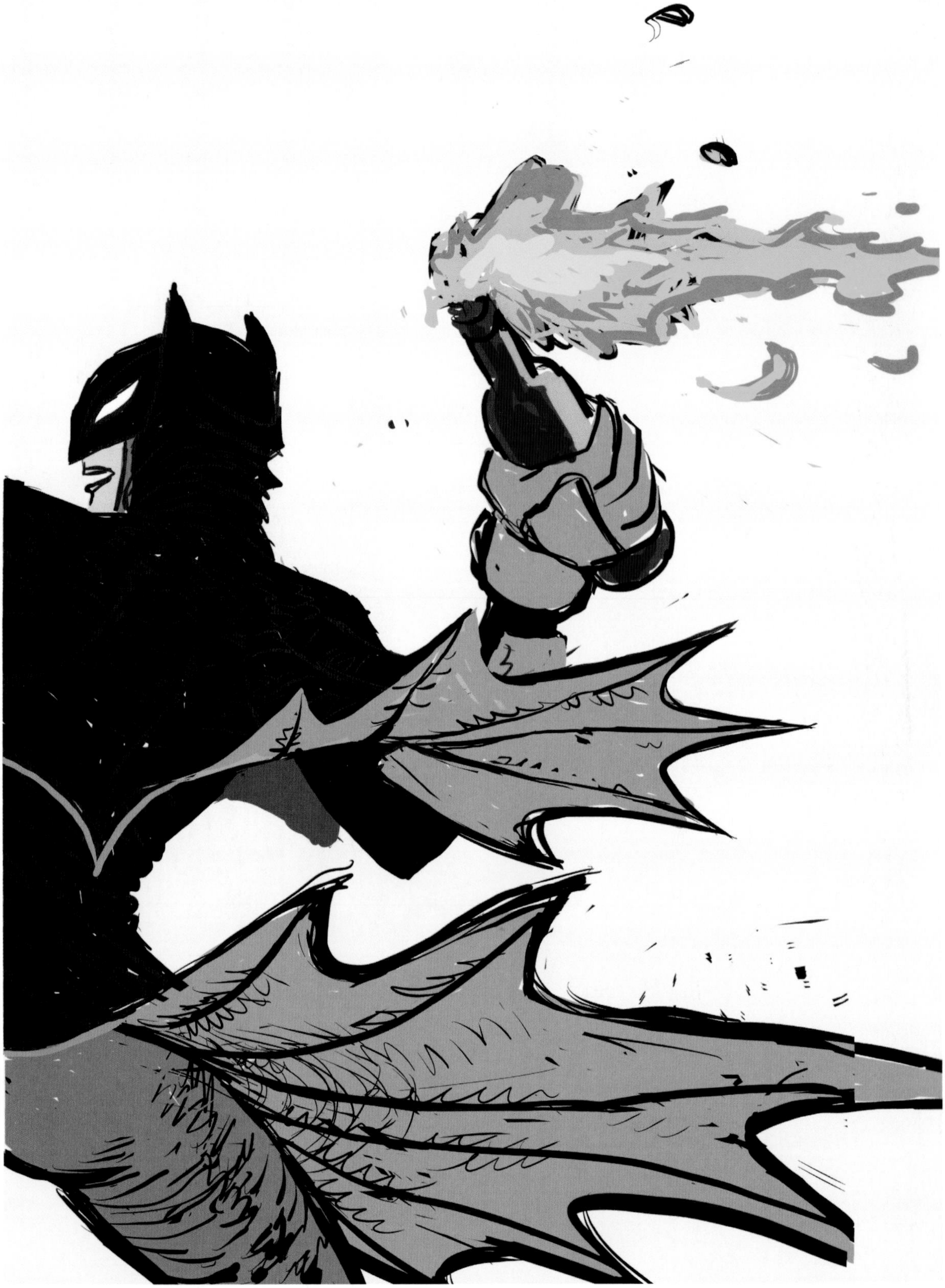

Layout of the polemic cover, which became a symbol of protest upon its release. Frank calls it the propaganda poster!